Daniel King is a Barrister (Lincoln's Inn) specialising in insurance law, personal injury, and civil fraud. As a former Solicitor (with Higher Rights of audience), his experience in the sector spans more than twenty years having worked for some of the most prominent national and international insurance law firms. He read law at the University of Newcastle before completing the Legal Practice Course at the Chester College of Law, Christleton.

Daniel appears in courts throughout England and Wales on a nigh on daily basis, often representing major blue chip insurers and their policyholders at trials and final hearings. He regularly advises insurers and lay clients alike in respect of indemnity issues and is an expert in the fields of insurance and reinsurance. Daniel acts for both Claimants and Defendants and his previous experience as a Solicitor means that he is ideally placed to advise on issues of indemnity at every stage of the litigation process from pre-issue all the way through to trial.

A Practical Guide to Indemnity Issues in Motor Claims

A Practical Guide to Indemnity Issues in Motor Claims

Daniel King LLB,
Barrister, Lincoln's Inn

Law Brief Publishing

Published 2025 by Law Brief Publishing, an imprint of Law Brief Publishing Ltd
30 The Parks
Minehead
Somerset
TA24 8BT

www.lawbriefpublishing.com

Paperback: 978-1-916698-73-4

To my family, my wife Sue, and my daughters, Grace and Eleanor

PREFACE

In my practice as a barrister, certainly within the realms of motor insurance law, the most common technical enquiry I have received over the years has been one revolving around issues of indemnity and insurer duties to satisfy claims. That really was reason enough to write this book and to hopefully deal with as many of those technical conundrums as possible Indemnity is a pervasive topic in motor claims but is one that can only rear its head fleetingly, which is why I believe many of us dealing in motor claims often struggle to find the answer to any given nuanced scenario (as they often are!) and I hope this book assists all of you in not only finding the correct solution, but doing so much more efficiently.

The framework of indemnity insurance underpinning motor claims in England and Wales is something of a fragile one often said to be in need of a greater degree of certainty. Re-written to comply with the Directives of their cousins in the EU, revised in a post-Brexit era, and subjected to reform and higher court jurisprudence setting new precedents, one could easily be forgiven for not being fully "up to date" with the status quo when it comes to the principle of indemnity.

Yet notwithstanding that, underpinning the framework is the governing principle of indemnity. That provides a level of assurance to all those unfortunate innocent victims of road traffic accidents to be sure of one certainty – that their claim will be met. In what circumstances, who by, and when it *may* not, form largely the theoretical and practical thesis of this book.

It is a consequence of natural justice that the law will ever evolve. It must do so to stay fit for purpose and in order to provide protection and freedoms to the very citizens of society it serves.

In recent years it is difficult to think of any other legal sector which has undergone quite so much reform as that of the insurance and personal injury one. Following the introduction of "the Whiplash Reforms"[1] those practicing in the area of motor claims have had to contend with reduced fee income and a sharp reduction in the volume of work as more operators in the area exit the market to seek what they perceive to be more profitable areas, as more cases enter into an Official Injury Claims Portal designed for litigants in person.

Of course many of these reforms have been driven by the insurance companies themselves, often following the introduction of legislative reform policies designed to reduce premiums and as a result of lobbying government using their considerable financial resources and influence.

In that sense it is perhaps more important than ever before to understand and interpret the rights and protections afforded by the insurance policy.

It is also just as important as a Claimant to know that the person to be sued is "good for the money", otherwise what is the point at all? In that sense, knowing if a tortfeasor is indemnified and by who, should be a pre-requisite to any litigation in motor claims. Conversely, those acting for Defendants really ought to know if they even have a liability at all, or if someone else should be picking up the tab.

Any driver of a car in England and Wales should be familiar with the concept of the policy of motor insurance and whilst such may be deemed a contractual matter, all too often such issues arise within the scope of a claim for damages as arising out of a road traffic accident.

The meat and drink of liability, causation, and quantum, will be all too familiar to most fee earners practising in this area, but often such issues can be overtaken by the need to understand the concept of indemnity. For that singular issue can, and will often be, determinative of whether a claim is even validly brought in the first place.

---

1 Introduced via the Civil Liability Bill 2018

The issues can be complex and many practitioners (whether claimant or defendant) may often need to seek advice in respect of matters such as

- The insurer has withdrawn indemnity from the defendant – who can I sue?
- What if there is no insurer?
- The Insurer is seeking rights of recovery against my client – what rights do they have?
- There are multiple insurers, which one is the correct defendant?
- The insurers are arguing about who owes a liability to the claimant – who should I sue?
- My insurer client doesn't think they have a liability for the claim – are they correct?
- Should liability for the claim devolve to the MIB?

This book is designed to act as a useful resource to all those involved in prosecuting or defending claims arising out of motor accidents in England and Wales, whether as a beginner or seasoned practitioner.

Many of the issues traversed in the book will hopefully provide you with the answer to a given technical query arising in respect of indemnity in motor claims and if it cannot assist in the avoidance of a litigation to a final hearing, it is hoped that in the alternative it will provide the correct guidance on how to approach tactical issues and argument at trial.

Navigating indemnity issues in motor claims can be technical and there is often a dearth of training on the subject matter for practitioners at all levels. The issues arising can often be rather bespoke in nature, which when taken together with the development of case law and legislation, mean resources such as this book will hopefully come in very useful when facing them head on, both in correspondence and at advocacy level. Similarly, the textbook cannot cover every eventuality in indemnity issues governing motor claims and given the bespoke nature of such issues on a case-by-case basis, the book cannot be seen as a substitute for legal advice and users are highly recommended to seek out advice and ensure that all materials and referenced legislation and case law is properly understood and researched accordingly.

Finally, the law is dynamic and subject to change either through legislative reform or the development of case law. This book is up to date as at the date of production and should be considered in light of any changes to the law.

The law cited within this text is presumed correct as at 14th February 2025.

Daniel King
February 2025

CONTENTS

PART ONE

THE INSURER'S LIABILITY

CHAPTER ONE

THE INDEMNITY PRINCIPLE

When applied in the most basic terms, the principle of indemnity ensures that another entity (often the insurer, but sometimes the MIB) will step into the shoes of the fault party/tortfeasor (often the driver, but sometimes the policyholder) to meet the claim of the wronged innocent party (that could be a driver of the other vehicle involved, innocent passenger, or pedestrian)[1].

That concept is widely accepted in common parlance as ones right to be placed back into the position that they would have been in – *restitutio in integrum* – but for the negligent breach of duty served upon them. The contract of motor insurance is just one way of ensuring a fault party can fulfil their tortious liability to "right the wrong" they served upon the third party unfortunate enough to have sustained a loss as a result of that actionable negligence.

In that sense, the contract of motor insurance is really a contract of indemnity, or a promise given by the motor insurer to its policyholder that it will meet the liability (provided of course that such a liability is covered – or insured – by the contract).

Since the introduction of the Road Traffic Act 1930 it has been a statutory requirement for all drivers of motor vehicles in England and Wales to have insurance covering them against "third party risks". That requirement is now entrenched within the Road Traffic Act 1988, which makes it implicit that any person who *"uses"* a motor vehicle "*on a road*

1 *British Cash and Parcel Conveyors Ltd v Lamson Store Service Co Ltd* [1908] 1 KB 1006 at 1014

(or other public place)"[2] must have in force a policy of motor insurance. Any person driving without such a policy is "*guilty of an offence*"[3].

Section 145 of the Act sets out a number of prescribed terms, which all policies coming into force must have. On the basis that those minimum requirements are met, the insurer will be contractually liable to indemnify the driver of the insured vehicle against any damage to the person or property of a third party. This is known as the "Insurer's duty to indemnify" the driver as against the claims brought by the party sustaining damage and/or losses.

Matters are not however as straight forward as they may seem, mainly due to the practice of issuing policies of motor insurance to individuals to drive specific motor vehicles (as opposed to being assigned to a vehicle insuring it for any, and all, who may drive it, for example), which is an idiosyncrasy of this jurisdiction. The result is that a person involved in an accident may have a host of potential insurers at their disposal for the purposes of suing for the recovery of their losses when involved in an accident in England and Wales.

By way of illustration, the following example encapsulates the mischief of the practice adopted in the UK:

Mr R is involved in a road traffic accident with *Mrs W, causing Mr R* to suffer personal injury and financial losses. The accident is the fault of *Mrs W*. However *Mrs W* is not specifically insured to drive the vehicle. She was driving the vehicle under the "driving other cars extension" on a separate policy she obtained in respect of her own vehicle. The vehicle she was driving belonged to *Mr W* and he had incepted a policy of motor insurance of his own for the vehicle involved in the accident.

---

2 s. 143(1)(a) of the Road Traffic Act 1988

3 s. 143(2) ibid.

In this scenario, Mr R has the option of recovering his losses from either Mr or Mrs W's insurance company. In most EU countries the answer would be more straightforward insofar as the vehicle involved would have a policy insuring the vehicle and that would be the party indemnifying Mrs W for the claim.

Quite *who* Mr R should pursue will be explored in more detail later in this chapter but such is the system of motor insurance in the UK, Mr R clearly has a choice. He might sue Mrs W's insurer who has provided her with a policy of insurance for another vehicle but which afforded her coverage to drive other cars; or alternatively he might sue Mr W's insurer which had issued a policy to Mr W in respect of the vehicle involved in the index accident. The situation becomes more complicated in the event that one, or both, of these insurers take the decision to withdraw indemnity from Mrs W. That may occur if the use of the vehicle at the material time of accident was not insured or, for example, the policy has been cancelled. Other reasons for withdrawal of indemnity may comprise non-disclosure of convictions (such as speeding penalties) or misrepresentation when the insurance contract was formed. For present purposes however, this chapter is primarily concerned only with the insurer's duty to indemnify, the exclusions and order of hierarchy of potential insurers will be explored in more detail later.

The task facing our hypothetical claimant – *Mr R* – and indeed many practitioners in the sector when it comes to deciding precisely which entity to pursue, is perhaps most eloquently articulated by Master Davison in his Judgment in the High Court case of **Advantage Insurance Company Ltd -v- Stoodley & Trinity Lane**[4], when he said

"When a road traffic accident occurs – even one involving only one vehicle – it is not unusual for more than one insurer to have a potential liability. This is partly a product of the fact that motor insurers in the UK insure the driver not the vehicle. (This stands in contrast to the position in the rest of the EU

4 [2018] EWHC 2135 (QB)

where it is usually the vehicle that is insured.) The potential liability of multiple insurers leads to disputes regarding their status. There exists what has come to be called the liability "tree" with the contractual insurer sitting at the top of the tree and the MIB Central Fund sitting at the bottom. As a general proposition (and looked at from the perspective of an insurer) if an insurer higher up the tree falls out, then liability to indemnify or satisfy a judgment will rest with the insurer immediately below."[5]

The Stoodley case is in fact a very similar scenario to that involving our own hypothetical example above. Mr Stoodley was behind the wheel of a BMW vehicle, which unfortunately left the carriageway and collided with a tree. Inside of that BMW were three passengers; Mr Hampton – the owner of the BMW, with whom he had incepted a policy of insurance for the BMW with Trinity Insurance (the second defendant); Mr Rogers who was fatally injured as a result of the accident; and finally, Mr Reed, who was catastrophically injured and brought a claim valued in the multi-millions. Mr Stoodley was not named on the policy issued to Mr Hampton by Trinity Insurance but he did have his own policy of motor insurance, issued by Advantage, in respect of a Vauxhall vehicle he owned. The case explored the battleground between Advantage (as contractual insurer to Mr Stoodley) and Trinity Insurance (as Road Traffic Act Insurer having issued a policy to Mr Hampton for the BMW).

In so doing, the very notion of the indemnity tree was born, Master Davison having planted the seeds for that particular sapling in his Judgment.

---

[5] Para 1 ibid.

Types of motor insurer

Before considering the hierarchy of insurers it will be helpful to understand the different types of insurer, most likely to fall into one of the following defined categories

- Contractual insurer – the insurer issuing a contract of insurance to the fault driver or in respect of the fault vehicle. In the vast majority of cases, this insurer will be the entity most likely to meet the liability of the driver to whom they issued the policy of motor insurance.

- S.148 Road Traffic Insurer or "the hybrid contractual insurer" – this type of insurer is reserved to those insurers in contract, usually an insurer that has issued a driver with a policy with "driving other cars" extension, but has withdrawn indemnity from the driver in contract but owes a contingent liability as modified pursuant to s.148 RTA 1988.

- S.151 Road Traffic Act Insurer – this term is often used to describe the insurer who have issued a policy of insurance covering the usage of the fault vehicle but have withdrawn indemnity (usually due to a breach of policy conditions, for example) but still retain a contingent liability to satisfy a claim pursuant to statute.

- The Article 75 insurer – this would be any insurer who have withdrawn indemnity from the driver of the fault vehicle and so cannot be contractual insurer but have also downgraded their status as Road Traffic Act Insurer, meaning they are only liable to the extent of the MIB Uninsured Drivers' Agreement.

- The Motor Insurers' Bureau – often the entity of "last resort" the MIB will step into the breach of the driver of the fault vehicle is uninsured or untraced (the result being that the Claimant has recourse pursuant via either the Uninsured Driver's Agreement or the Untraced Driver's Agreement). Such is the nature of insurance premiums a small portion of each is donated to the MIB to underpin that risk to all road users that the fault driver may be uninsured or untraced and thereby providing a safety net for all innocent victims that their loss will be met even in one of those two unfortunate scenarios.

RTA Insurer vs Contractual Insurer

Before we scrutinise the order of insurers or liable parties on the indemnity tree of hierarchy it is well worth considering the difference between a "Road Traffic Act Insurer" and a "contractual insurer" and who, if either of those entities, is the insurer with the liability to meet a claim.

The Road Traffic Act Insurer is the insurer which has issued the policy of motor insurance in respect of the fault vehicle (so to take the Stoodley case, that would be Trinity Insurance). The contingent liability to satisfy any Judgment so obtained against the fault party is laid down by statute within section 151 of the Road Traffic Act 1988.

The contractual insurer is the insurer which has issued a policy of motor insurance to the driver of the fault vehicle involved in the accident, but which does not expressly provide a coverage for that specific vehicle within the policy of insurance ie. the policy was issued to the fault driver for another vehicle, not involved, which means the fault driver was driving the vehicle under the "driving other cars" extension on the policy (as Mr Stoodley did per his policy with Advantage Insurance).

Without delving into the correct mechanism of how to sue either of these parties, that is to say, what the cause of action is, for present purposes one should understand which of these insurers trumps the other when it comes to the liability to indemnify the claim.

The conflict was explored further in the case of ***Legal & General v. Drake Insurance [1992] QB 887***, which shall be scrutinised in further detail in the following chapters.

As Master Davison explained, and as is now commonly accepted in civil claims by the judiciary, the contractual insurer is the entity at the top of the tree for indemnity purposes.

Whilst further clarification is to be expected to come in higher court jurisprudence on this point, and the order of indemnity is to be reconsidered on a case-by-case basis, for now at least one should work on the basis that the contractual insurer will be first in line to meet any claim where there are would be multiple insurers in play.

CHAPTER TWO

THE TREE OF HIERARCHY

The High Court considered the hierarchy of insurers in the case of **Advantage Insurance Company Ltd -v- Stoodley & Trinity Lane** and this chapter is designed to impart rationale behind that decision and thereby afford understanding of why the order of hierarchy is as it is.

The effect of the hierarchy is such that the potential liability falls from the top of the tree downwards so that the potential insurer or entity highest up the tree bears the responsibility of indemnity.

If that particular insurer is not deemed responsible in law to meet the liability then the claim will pass to the next branch down the tree.

The principle underpinning that system is in order to ensure that no innocent victim of a road traffic accident in England and Wales is left uncompensated, as should be the case in any modern and developed society.

Whilst the tree of hierarchy is commonly adopted by practitioners and courts alike it can be subject to challenge.

(i) The Contractual Insurer

Perched atop the tree of hierarchy is that entity we call the Contractual Insurer.

The contractual insurer will often be that insurer providing a full indemnity to its insured driver under the validly incepted policy of motor insurance. That means that the insurer will meet the claim presented to its insured driver in full without exception.

The contractual insurer will usually be the insurer that has issued a policy of motor insurance to an individual to drive a specific vehicle, whether that be the fault vehicle involved, or another vehicle meaning that the fault driver was driving the vehicle under his driving other car extension on the policy.

There will have been no breach of the policy of motor insurance and the insurer will meet the claims against it directly or as against its insured driver. The driver may be named on a policy of insurance issued to someone else as a named driver, or he may have his own policy of insurance permitting him to drive other vehicles.

When the insured driver is able to retain a contractual indemnity from his motor insurer the Claimant may choose to sue one or both of the insured driver and insurance company. They can do so directly against the insurer pursuant to **Regulation 3 of The European Communities (Rights Against Insurers) Regulations 2002**.

An individual's entitlement to directly pursue a cause of action against an insurer is set out as follows within the regulations:

> *Right of action*
>
> *3.—(1) Paragraph (2) of this regulation applies where an entitled party has a cause of action against an insured person in tort or (as the case may be) delict, and that cause of action arises out of an accident.*
>
> *(2) Where this paragraph applies, the entitled party may, without prejudice to his right to issue proceedings against the insured person, issue proceedings against the insurer which issued the policy of insurance relating to the insured vehicle, and that insurer shall be directly liable to the entitled party to the extent that he is liable to the insured person.*

The situation becomes problematic if indemnity is withdrawn from the policyholder, or if there is an exclusion meaning that coverage under the policy is not granted (exceptions could include driving outside of the prescribed use). For example, if a policy is incepted for social, domestic and pleasure use of a vehicle only, but the insured driver has an accident whilst driving in the course of his employment or on the commute, that usage is not covered by the policy.

There are then more extreme examples, such as using the policy whilst in pursuit of criminal activity, or even whilst "racing the vehicle" for instance. Neither of these situations would be covered under most contracts of motor insurance resulting in indemnity being withdrawn.

Other more common examples giving rise to contractual insurance being withdrawn from an otherwise insured driver are explored later in this book but can include misrepresentation, failure to co-operate, amongst other breaches of the policy of insurance.

(ii) The s.148 Road Traffic Act Insurer – (aka "the Hybrid contractual insurer")

In the event that the contractual insurer has withdrawn indemnity from its insured person in contract (either for misrepresentation or non-co-operation etc) then the next insurer further down the tree of indemnity will be what has come to be known as "the hybrid insurer".

The definition was coined by Master Davison in the High Court in the case of Advantage Insurance Co Ltd -v- Stoodley & Trinity Lane Insurance Co. as pertaining to a contractual insurer that had withdrawn indemnity from its insured driver but nonetheless retained a contingent liability pursuant to contract as modified by section 148 of the Road Traffic Act 1988.

In the Stoodley case, Advantage (as contractual insurer of Mr Stoodley having insured him to drive his Vauxhall vehicle – he was driving the doomed BMW under his "driving other cars" extension on that policy) had sought a declaration that it was not liable to indemnify Mr Stoodley by reason of them withdrawing indemnity under the policy of motor insurance. It was their case that indemnity should fall squarely at the door of Trinity Lane Insurance, who had issued a policy to Mr Hampton insuring his BMW that Mr Stoodley was driving.

Advantage Insurance did so on grounds that they had withdrawn indemnity from Mr Stoodley because he had failed to comply with the terms of his policy requiring him to report the accident and co-operate with their investigations. Mr Stoodley was also later convicted of causing death by dangerous driving whilst over the legal limit for alcohol.

It is accepted legal principle that Advantage have the entitlement in contract to withdraw indemnity from Mr Stoodley and avoid the policy, but the position is modified by s.148 RTA 1988 as follows:

> *"148.— Avoidance of certain exceptions to policies or securities.*
>
> *(5) A condition in a policy or security issued or given for the purposes of this Part of this Act providing—*
>
> *(a) that no liability shall arise under the policy or security, or*
>
> *(b) that any liability so arising shall cease,*
>
> *in the event of some specified thing being done or omitted to be done after the happening of the event giving rise to a claim under the policy or security, shall be of no effect in connection with such liabilities as are required to be covered by a policy under section 145 of this Act.*
>
> *(6) Nothing in subsection (5) above shall be taken to render void any provision in a policy or security requiring the person insured or secured to pay to the insurer or the giver of the security any sums which the latter may have become liable to pay under the policy or*

> *security and which have been applied to the satisfaction of the claims of third parties."*

Advantage argued that the driving other car extension that Mr Stoodley sought to rely upon as affording him coverage was not a liability covered under s.145 of the RTA 1988, therefore rendering s.148 of no relevance.

s.145 stipulates the following:

> *"145 (3)(a) the policy must insure such person, persons or classes of persons as may be specified in the policy in respect of any liability which may be incurred by him or them in respect of the death of or bodily injury to any person or damage to property caused by, or arising out of, the use of the vehicle on a road or other public place in Great Britain and (aa) must, in the case of a vehicle normally based in the territory of another Member State, insure him or them in respect of any civil liability which may be incurred by him or them as a result of an event related to the use of the vehicle in Great Britain if (i) according to the law of that territory, he or they would be required to be insured in respect of a civil liability which would arise under that law as a result of that event if the place where the vehicle was used when the event occurred were in that territory, and (ii) the cover required by that law would be higher than that required by paragraph (a) above ...".*

Advantage had joined Trinity Lane Insurance into proceedings since if their argument was successful, in avoiding the contract of insurance with Mr Stoodley, it was inevitable that Trinity Lane Insurance would meet the claim as RTA Insurer of the BMW.

The argument of Advantage rested almost entirely on an interpretation of the words "...arising out of the use of the vehicle on the road" as canvassed within s.145. It was their case that "the vehicle" was to be construed as meaning the vehicle insured under the policy (the requisite vehicle under their policy being the Vauxhall as opposed to the fault BMW involved in the accident).

Master Davison disagreed with the argument ventilated by Advantage on three key grounds, summarised as follows:

- The purpose of s.143 and 145 was to warn the drivers of cars against driving without insurance since to do so would be committing an offence – Mr Stoodley was entitled to rely on the Certificate of Insurance issued to him by Advantage "as stating that he could lawfully drive another car"[6].

- Once Mr Stoodley had started to drive the BMW under the driving other car extension on his policy with Advantage Insurance "that car became the vehicle insured for the purposes of the policy and "the vehicle" for the purposes of section 145(3)" since the policy incepted with Advantage offered cover for more than one vehicle[7].

- To interpret the driving other car extension as being outwith the meaning of "the vehicle" within s.145 RTA 1988 "would lead to the absurd result that a driver using another car under the DOC provisions of their policy of insurance would be committing a criminal offence under section 143(2) RTA 1988" when the contrary was the reality of the situation, the certificate of insurance issued by Advantage complying with that rule and thus ensuring the car was being legally driven.

Whilst it is still open to interpretation and there have been some other lower court decisions going the other way, resulting in the contractual insurer escaping indemnity completely, the ruling of Master Davison affirms the contractual insurer's place at the top of the tree of hierarchy in the first instance as insurer in contract, but even if that contract is

6 Paragraph 22, [2018] EWHC 2135 (QB)

7 Paragraph 23, ibid.

subsequently voided, in their capacity as the newly born cousin second in line – "the hybrid contractual insurer".

(iii) S.151 Road Traffic Act Insurer

In the event that an insurer is entitled to absolve itself of a contractual liability to its insured and thus withdraw indemnity, the claimant should look to the next branch down on the tree, where they would find the s.151 Road Traffic Act Insurer.

Notwithstanding that there may have been the sort of breaches of policy giving rise to a withdrawal of contractual indemnity under the policy of motor insurance, an insurer may still find themselves on the hook pursuant to the statutory entitlement canvassed within The Road Traffic Act 1988.

An insurer falling into this particular category would, subject to some narrow exceptions, retain a contingent liability to satisfy any Judgment so obtained by a Claimant against the driver of the insured vehicle against which the policy was issued in respect of pursuant to **section 151 of the Road Traffic Act 1988, "Duty of Insurers to satisfy judgment against persons insured",** which provides as follows:

> *"(1) This section applies where, after a policy is issued for the purposes of this Part of this Act, a judgment to which this subsection applies is obtained.*
>
> *(2) Subsection (1) above applies to judgments relating to a liability with respect to any matter where liability with respect to that matter is required to be covered by a policy of insurance under section 145 of this Act and either—*
>
> *(a) it is a liability covered by the terms of the policy, and the judgment is obtained against any person who is insured by the policy, or*

> *(b) it is a liability, other than an excluded liability, which would be so covered if the policy insured all persons and the judgment is obtained against any person other than one who is insured by the policy"*

It follows therefore that even in a situation where the driver of the vehicle is not named on the policy of motor insurance, the Road Traffic Act insurer will retain a contingent liability to satisfy any Judgment so obtained against that person as arising out of the negligent usage of the insured vehicle (s.151(2)(b), *ibid.*).

The liability of the Road Traffic Act insurer is further entrenched by virtue of the provisions of s.151(5) of the 1988 Act, when it explicitly sets out the contingent liability of a Road Traffic Act insurer to meet a Judgment even in a situation where the insurer has avoided or cancelled the contract of motor insurance, as follows:

> *(5)Notwithstanding that the insurer may be entitled to avoid or cancel, or may have avoided or cancelled, the policy... , he must, subject to the provisions of this section, pay to the persons entitled to the benefit of the judgment—*
>
> *(a) as regards liability in respect of death or bodily injury, any sum payable under the judgment in respect of the liability, together with any sum which, by virtue of any enactment relating to interest on judgments, is payable in respect of interest on that sum,*
>
> *(b) as regards liability in respect of damage to property, any sum required to be paid under subsection (6) below, and*
>
> *(c) any amount payable in respect of costs.*

The purpose of this provision of course is to ensure that the innocent victims of the negligence of those insured to drive still have some recourse against insurers notwithstanding that there may be some material breach of policy between driver and insurer. Otherwise the Road Traffic Act insurer would have more or less the same exit from indemnity as the contractual insurer, which is the point to be made, this is a statutory liability to prevent the mischief of an insurer escaping under contract.

The interplay between Contractual Insurer and Road Traffic Act insurer and whether either, or both, should carry the liability for settling a claim against a potential insured has been the source of litigation in the higher courts. Whether or not a contribution could be procured from one insurer to another was considered in higher court jurisprudence in the cases of ***Legal & General v. Drake Insurance*** [1992] **QB** 887 and ***EagleStar Ltd v Provincial Insurance Plc [1994] 1 A.C. 130 (PC).*** In both cases there was apparently a double insurance insofar as two insurers were found liable to indemnify the driver of the fault vehicle. It was held that an equitable right to contribution arose between two insurers, which was to be determined in accordance with the insurer's liability to its own insured as at the date of the loss. It is therefore axiomatic that if a Road Traffic Act Insurer has no contractual liability to its insured or the driver of the insured vehicle, whereas the Contractual Insurer does retain such a liability, then the Contractual Insurer will be obliged to meet all of the claim. Additionally it would be expected that the Road Traffic Act Insurer pursued a claim in contribution pursuant to the 1988 Act, or equity, against the Contractual Insurer.

There is a lack of recent authority on this point and it is expected that challenges may soon be made to that concept of hierarchy but until such time as there is, one should tread carefully on contribution claims between insurers and carefully consider the policy wording.

(iv) Article 75 Insurer

Following down the tree of hierarchy beneath Road Traffic Act Insurer will follow Article 75 Insurer on the branch below.

An Article 75 Insurer is effectively the Road Traffic Act Insurer who has successfully managed to obtain a declaration reducing their status to that of Article 75 Insurer, which essentially limits their liability to one equivalent to the Motor Insurers' Bureau would be under either of the Untraced Driver's Agreement or the Uninsured Driver's Agreement.

As an insurer in the business of incepting policies of motor insurance in England and Wales, it is compulsory to also be a member of the Motor Insurers' Bureau, which means they are members of the same articles of association.

Article 75(2) of the Articles of Association of the Motor Insurers' Bureau defines an Article 75 Insurer, for present purposes, as follows:

> ***"the Member who for the time of the event which gave rise to a Road Traffic Act Liability was providing any insurance (other than by reason only of a driving other vehicle clause) in respect of the vehicle from the use of which the liability of the judgment debtor arose."***

An Article 75 Insurer may therefore be an insurer who has issued a policy of motor insurance in respect of a vehicle, which was not being used in accordance within the policy coverage. That may be a stolen vehicle, a vehicle which was being used for commercial purposes when the coverage only extended to social and domestic purposes.

One should note that a contractual insurer who has a potential indemnity by reason of the insured driving a vehicle under the "driving other vehicle" extension of his policy with them cannot downgrade to Article 75 Insurer. Instead their escape is to be found in policy avoidance by reason of the more straightforward breach of contract terms, which will then lead to the potential liability passing down the tree of hierarchy to Road Traffic Act Insurer and so on.

The incidence of insurer's downgrading their status to Article 75 Insurer is now far less prolific than it once was owing to the implementation of The Motor Vehicles (Compulsory Insurance) (Miscellaneous Amendments) Regulations 2019. Those Regulations amended s.152 of the Road Traffic Act 1988 insofar as the insurer's right to cancel or void a policy of motor insurance and thereby apply for a declaration was removed if done after the occurrence of an accident from 1st November 2019 onwards. Prior to then insurers were entitled, and would often, cancel policies of motor insurance on grounds of misrepresentation by policyholders even if that misrepresentation came to light after the happening of an accident and accordingly, with hindsight pull the rug from under the feet of its insured driver. Following the 2019 Regulations being implemented an insurer can only seek to avoid its s.151 liability under the Act if it has a) cancelled the policy of motor insurance before the accident has taken place, b) obtained a declaration to downgrade its status on grounds of misrepresentation before the accident, or c) the use of the insured vehicle at the material time was one not permitted by the policy of motor insurance and thus outwith the indemnity provided under contract.

As expected, and as will be explored in more detail later, that has naturally led to a number of arguments as to the definition of "use" within the meaning of the policy wording as more insurers look to extract themselves out of positions of owing indemnity by virtue of the use not being one covered in contract.

So it follows that if the insurer is able to obtain declaratory relief under one of the aforementioned three exceptions to its liability as Road Traffic Act Insurer, it will become the Article 75 insurer, owing a more limited liability to indemnity the would be claimant.

(v) The Motor Insurers' Bureau

Finally, found hanging upon the lowest branch of the liability tree of hierarchy, one will find the Motor Insurers' Bureau – otherwise known as "the insurer of last resort".

The Motor Insurers' Bureau may meet the claim and indemnify a driver in one of two limited scenarios, that is if the driver is either untraced or uninsured.

Both scenarios are governed by the Motor Insurers' Bureau agreements and contain a number of exceptions to the right of recovery.

In addition, the costs of litigation against the MIB are very limited.

The case of Cameron v Hussain[8] in the Supreme Court has provided helpful guidance on the correct procedure to follow when drivers are untraced (which is a common occurrent in hit and run type accidents, or those were drivers make off without providing details at the scene).

Summary

In light of the various places an insurer may come to rest in the tree of hierarchy, the importance of establishing status cannot be overstated.

For reasons which will be amplified upon in the chapters to come, the status within that hierarchy can have significant implications for the purposes of identifying the correct cause of action, the remedy sought, and the extent of an insurer's liability.

The ruling of Master Davison in *Stoodley* is welcomed in that it provides much need clarity on the status of a contractual insurer that has withdrawn indemnity from an insured.

What is apparent from that particular judgment is that any arguments in respect of indemnity and / or contribution should be raised within the index proceedings concerning the primary action. Whether that is in a

8 [2019] UKSC 6

Part 20 claim for contribution and / or declaratory relief as to an insurer's liability in indemnity, or in the Defence.

CHAPTER THREE

THE CONTINGENT LIABILITY PER S.151 OF RTA 1988

The contingent liability of an insurer to satisfy a judgment debt against *any* person driving a motor vehicle in respect of which that insurer issued a policy of motor insurance is implicit within s.151(5) of the Road Traffic Act 1988. The effect of the provision is to require insurers to satisfy judgments obtained against drivers of vehicles insured, even if that driver was not named on the policy of motor insurance issued by it, provided that the usage of the vehicle at the material time was one covered by the policy (see s.151(2)(b)).

The liability remains even if the driver of the vehicle was not the holder of a valid driving licence at the time (s.151(3)).

That is a liability arising even when an insurer purports to have, or could, cancel the contract of insurance under s.152 RTA 1988.

There are however a number of mandatory requirements to be met a pre-requisite for an insurer to be liable pursuant to s.151, which are set out as follows:

- The insurance certificate must have been delivered to the insured per s.147 RTA 1988.

- There has been a Judgment obtained for a sum of money either against the person insured by the policy, or a person who would have been insured were the policy to have covered "all persons".

- The liability is covered by the policy (that liability could be for any sum in respect of death or bodily injury, property damage, and / or an amount in costs up to the amount of £1.2 million[9]).

The effect of the RTA liability pursuant to s.151 is such that, provided the terms above are met, and none of the exclusions within s.152 are engaged, that an insurer is required by statute to satisfy a Judgment even in the event that:

- There has been a breach of the policy by the insured.
- The vehicle has been stolen.
- The driver of the vehicle was not the holder of a valid driving licence.
- The policy was incepted by misrepresentation or on a false premise.
- The policy premiums were not paid on time or at all.

The options open to an insurer in the situations described above are explored in further detail in this book, which may comprise an action for recovery against an insured (Part 5), or perhaps an application to downgrade to Article 75 (Part 4).

However, for present purposes it is important not to lose sight of the very wide capture s.151 liability has in its barest form as a tool for compelling insurers to satisfy judgments in a very broad number of contexts.

9 The limit was increased from £1m with effect from 31 December 2016 by the Motor Vehicles (Compulsory Insurance) Regulations 2016.

CHAPTER FOUR

THE CONTRACTUAL INSURER AND "DRIVING OTHER CAR (DOC)" EXTENSIONS

As should now be clear from the preceding chapters, the contractual insurer is one which will afford indemnity to the insured driver pursuant to the policy of motor insurance. That will also allow a third party to pursue an insurer directly (as sole defendant if necessary) pursuant to the European Community (Rights Against Insurers) Regulations 2002.

A number of insurance policies do however seek to exclude coverage in various situations and when insurers are pursued under the regulations following accidents in which one or more of these exclusions are engaged, insurers will often seek to withdraw indemnity from the insured driver.

Some common examples of exclusions from coverage will include mis-representations made pre-inception of the policy, failing to keep the insurer updated on a material fact (such as motoring offences or modifications to the vehicle), going above a cap on mileage, driving under the influence of drugs or alcohol, or failing to report an accident and / or comply with an investigation of a claim made against the policy.

Whilst the contractual insurer may seek to withhold or withdraw indemnity on grounds that one or more of these exclusions are operative, it is worth bearing in mind that many of the exclusions often contained within the policy of motor insurance are specifically prohibited by s.148 of the Road Traffic Act 1988.

Another contentious area is that of the "driving other cars" extension permitting insured drivers to drive other vehicles even though that vehicle is not specifically mentioned on their policy and also when they are not named on the policy issued for the vehicle they drive under that extension. The by product of that coverage is that it often results in a "double" insurance of the vehicle by virtue of the driving other car extension on the driver's policy and also via the insurance policy incepted in respect of the vehicle being driven.

For a long tome the contractual insurers would, in the event that there was an exclusion to coverage in the policy, seek to escape liability by passing on the indemnity liability to the insurer of the car (the RTA insurer). However, as explored in Chapter 2, the ruling of Master Davison in the *Stoodley* case has meant that the contractual insurer issuing a policy to the person insured to drive other cars under their own policy has a modified contractual liability to indemnify the insured driver pursuant to s.148 of the Road Traffic Act 1988.

The reasoning behind that principle is that the certificate of insurance permitting driving other cars is one issued in compliance with s.143 and s.145 of the RTA 1988. It must therefore follow that the correct construction of the wording "insured car" within the meaning of s.145 RTA 1988 is that car the insured person is driving under the driving other car extension on his policy, since that policy expressly permits him to legally drive another car (not specifically identified) in accordance with the coverage afforded by the insurance certificate. In that way, it is possible for a contractual insurer to retain a contingent liability to satisfy a Judgment pursuant to s.151 RTA 1988 even in the situation where they have withdrawn indemnity. That status is often referred to as "the hybrid contractual insurer".

Such an insurer status will trump that of a s.151 Road Traffic Act Insurer as defined within Chapter 3, which is normally the insurer of the fault vehicle, being driven by a person not named on that policy of insurance. In that sense such an insurer cannot be termed the contractual insurer since they have no contractual liability to the fault driver.

CHAPTER FIVE

THE MOTOR INSURERS' BUREAU

Liability to indemnify the fault driver of a vehicle will devolve to the Motor Insurers' Bureau when the driver is uninsured or untraced.

The Uninsured Driver's Agreement [2015][10]

Dealing first with the "uninsured driver" it is important to be precise on that definition since as has already been set out, insurers will often withdraw indemnity from drivers of insured vehicles for a number of reasons, and in that sense may result in that driver being classed as "uninsured". However, as prescribed by the Road Traffic Act 1988, such insurers will still retain a contingent liability to satisfy a Judgment so obtained against their insured. In those situations, liability will not devolve to the Motor Insurers' Bureau.

For these purposes therefore, it is important to understand that an uninsured driver for the purposes of the Uninsured Driver's Agreement, is the driver of a car that was not insured in either contract, or pursuant to s.143 of the Road Traffic Act 1988 (the result being that there can be no Article 75 insurer either). It will be a vehicle completely free from compulsory insurance.

The agreement places an obligation on the Motor Insurers' Bureau to satisfy claims subject to a number of conditions, exceptions, and limitations, set out therein.

[10] Updated by the Supplementary Uninsured Drivers Agreement [2017]

Some of the exceptions to the Motor Insurers' Bureau's obligation to satisfy a claim include but are not limited to the following:

- Accidents involving crown vehicles

- Vehicles that are not required to have a contract of insurance in accordance with s.144 of the Road Traffic Act 1988.

- Where the Claimant is entitled to an indemnity from another person or entity (such as their own insurer for example in respect of their own vehicle damage, which may be covered under a fully comprehensive motor policy). Such losses are often termed "subrogated losses", which the Motor Insurers' Bureau will not compensate for. The exception to this rule is if the other recourse is to the Criminal Injuries. Compensation Authority ("CICA") for example, an injury sustained by someone who is the victim of a crime (such as an uninsured person using a vehicle as a weapon).

- Passengers allowing themselves to be transported in a vehicle they knew, or ought to have known, was stolen.

The Untraced Driver's Agreement [2017]

The Motor Insurers' Bureau will indemnify the driver of a vehicle giving rise to liabilities where that driver is untraced or cannot be identified.

The conditions a Claimant need satisfy to pursue this avenue of recovery are very strict and should be considered very carefully before an application is made to the Motor Insurers' Bureau using the MIB's prescribed Claim Form. Such applications will be considered by the Motor Insurers' Bureau in respect of causation and quantum and a decision referred to the technical committee of the Motor Insurers' Bureau. Individuals may have the right to appeal depending on the outcome and grounds of appeal. The Motor Insurers' Bureau will carry out its own investigations in terms of the claim and shall require a heavy burden of co-operation from the claimant in those enquiries.

Previously, all prospective Claimants were required to have reported the accident involving an untraced or unidentified fault driver (normally having fled the scene without exchanging details) to the police. However the mandatory reporting requirement has now been amended to apply only when the Claimant has been required to do so by the Motor Insurers' Bureau[11]. Whilst it would still be best practice and highly recommended for Claimants to report incidents of involving unidentified drivers to the police, the abolition of this as a mandatory requirement is expected to present less obstacle to Claimants pursuing claims under the Untraced Driver's Agreement.

The Motor Insurers' Bureau also require a Claimant to demonstrate that they have sustained "significant personal injury" if pursuing claims under this agreement. As to what is defined by "significant" is set out as including claims involving death, two nights of in-patient hospital treatment, or 3 sessions of out-patient treatment.

The Motor Insurers' Bureau's contribution towards legal costs for pursuing claims under the Untraced Driver's Agreement remain relatively low and are calculated on a stepped basis depending on the level of the award. The contribution amounts to legal costs is set out within section 21 of the agreement (by way of illustration £450 is the fee entitlement for claims settled at awards less than £10,000; and £700 for claims awarded more than £10,000 but less than £25,000).

[11] Paragraph 10(4)(a)(b) of the Untraced Driver's Agreement 2017

PART TWO

IDENTIFYING THE CORRECT DEFENDANT & CAUSE OF ACTION

CHAPTER SIX

THE CLAIMANT'S CHOICE

The Claimant has it within their gift to pursue the defendant it wishes. Ordinarily, that should be the party that the Claimant believes is the most culpable, or alternatively, the party that is likely to deal with their claim most efficiently and lucratively.

That will often be a matter of advice to be imparted to the Claimant by their appointed legal representative and will ultimately depend upon the outcome of various enquiries to be made.

The potential defendants a claimant may opt to prosecute their claim against include:

- The fault driver
- The owner of the vehicle (for example, the driver's employer)
- The contractual insurer of the driver
- The RTA insurer issuing a policy in respect of the vehicle
- The Motor Insurers' Bureau

It is of significant importance to the Claimant to identify the defendant to be sued at the earliest opportunity. Litigation is costly and once proceedings are issued can take many months, if not years, to come to trial.

But moreover, identifying the Defendant to be sued will afford the requisite enquiries to be made as to the indemnity status, thereby forearming the Claimant in respect of what the cause of action is likely to be.

The fault driver

The most obvious and straightforward way of prosecuting a claim arising out of a motor claim is for the Claimant to issue proceedings against the fault driver (otherwise known as the tortfeasor).

Those proceedings would normally be issued following exhaustion of the relevant pre-action protocols (which would axiomatically involve the insurer of the fault driver being identified given that many personal injury claims now require lodgement of a claim on a Ministry of Justice type portal depending on the value). That would have the effect of "flagging" the existence of a claim to the relevant insurer but in the event the claim is not responded to or was to leave the process for any reason (not the subject of this book), and in the absence of any clarification of the indemnity position, sometimes requesting that an insurer be included in proceedings by reason of indemnity being withheld, the proceedings could conceivable be issued against the fault driver only and served on them directly.

The obvious benefit of issuing directly against the fault driver only to the Claimant are obvious. It is as simplistic as it gets and ensures a Particulars of Claim simplistic in brevity for that is a claim brought in the tort of negligence. The individual Defendant as fault driver, if insured, ought to refer the matter to his insurance company for dealing. But as is sometimes the case, they might not respond to the proceedings served upon them creating an opportunity for a Claimant to request Judgment in default pursuant to Civil Procedure Rule 12 (being a Judgment in default of an Acknowledgement of Service or Defence).

The drawbacks of issuing solely against the fault driver can however unintentionally lead to unnecessary and unintended delays. In the event that a claim is not referred to an insurer by the fault driver may of itself give rise to indemnity issues being raised. Some insurance companies may even rely on that omission or failure on the fault driver's part not to flag the issuing of proceedings against them, for which the insurer has a contingent liability to satisfy pursuant to s.151 of the RTA 1988, as a reason in itself to withdraw indemnity.

Another potential pitfall for Claimants might also rear its head in the event that indemnity has been withdrawn from the fault driver, and an insurer therefore requires its inclusion in the proceedings anyway.

It may therefore be preferable for Claimants to make enquiries with the relevant insurer at the earliest point to establish the indemnity position and thereby avoid delays in the long run.

The relevant insurer

The Claimant may alternatively, or in addition to the fault driver, issue proceedings against the relevant insurer.

In order to establish the identity of the insurer of the fault vehicle, the Claimant's solicitor should conduct a search of the Motor Insurer's Database ("MID"). The MID is a database holding data for all vehicles insured in England and Wales and works so that the relevant date of accident and vehicle registration is used to identify the relevant insurer to the vehicle.

The problem of solely relying on a MID search is that it will not necessarily reveal the identity of the contractual insurer (since the contractual insurer may well be an insurer that has issued a policy of motor insurance to the driver of the fault vehicle but in respect of another vehicle). Accordingly, the identity of that contractual insurer will not show on a MID search as being the relevant insurer of the fault vehicle.

Claimant's and their representatives should therefore tread carefully when considering whether or not the relevant insurer has in fact been identified.

Take the following scenario as illustrative of the problems facing Claimants in identifying the most proximate insurer:

A plausible scenario would be, for example, where the Claimant is involved in an accident with Mr H, who is driving his friend, Mr G's vehicle, which Mr G has insurance for with the RTA Insurer. Mr H is not named on the RTA Insurer's policy of insurance but he is covered to drive other vehicles under another policy of insurance issued in respect of his own vehicle under the "driving other cars extension".

The Claimant and Mr H exchange details at the scene but nothing is said of the identity of insurers (as is sometime the case if parties do not readily know the name of their insurer or only know the broker / brand name etc).

The Claimant sustains an injury and financial loss and so instructs a local firm of solicitors to pursue Mr H to recover damages.

The Claimant's Solicitor carry out a MID search which reveals the RTA Insurer, being Mr G's insurer, as the relevant insurer and pursue them accordingly.

This is an all too common scenario encountered in day to day practice leading unfortunately to delays, or in the worst case scenario, claims being struck out by reason of pursuing the wrong cause of action against insurers.

Mr G's insurer may well be the RTA Insurer of the fault vehicle, but as was identified in accordance with the tree of hierarchy, such an insurer rank only third in line as the most proximate insurer.

There is of course nothing to stop the Claimant from pursuing Mr G's insurer for their losses, but that is likely to lead to delays given that the RTA Insurer likely will not provide indemnity to Mr H (he is not named on their policy of insurance), thereby rendering their addition to proceedings as a mandatory requirement before settlement, in addition to a Judgment first being required to have been obtained against Mr H directly (in order to comply with the conditions of s.151 RTA 1988).

The most efficient and pragmatic way of pursuing this claim would therefore be by way of identifying the contractual insurer of Mr H. That information could be procured by a direct approach, or Mr G's insurer may even make their own enquiries and release that information, but if neither of those avenues produce any meaningful result, the Claimant may be required to make an application for pre-action disclosure of the name of Mr H's insurer.

CHAPTER SEVEN

PRE-ACTION DISCLOSURE APPLICATIONS

By its very nature, a Pre-Action Disclosure Application (or a "PAD Application) is made pre-issue of proceedings in personal injury claims ordinarily when the Claimant is seeking further information or to clarify a position in order to fully consider their case and take the step of formally bringing a claim at court.

The Pre-Action Disclosure Application is a useful tool in a prospective Claimant's armoury to be able to compel a fault driver or would be defendant to disclose details of their insurance (if any). The application is just as useful against insurance companies in order to procure the details of a fault driver in a situation where the fault driver is unidentified and a MID search has revealed the identity of the RTA Insurer of the fault vehicle.

Prior to the issuing of a Pre-Action Disclosure Application a Claimant should usually give a Defendant the opportunity to respond without the need of making an application and solicitors acting on the Claimant's behalf would be well advised to set out verbatim precisely what information, clarification, or extent of information is being requested and for what purpose. In the event that an unsatisfactory, or no response is forthcoming from a Defendant, then the PAD application should be made and all relevant correspondence annexed to it in support.

The relevant rule governing these applications can be found at Civil Procedure Rule 31.16 and confirms that the application must be supported by evidence and made before proceedings have started. The rule also makes clear that an order may only be made where both parties are likely to be party to subsequent proceedings.

The advantage of making such applications is the potential time and money it could save in the long term should the requisite information and evidence be forthcoming thereby allowing narrowing of issues and the Claimant to identify who to pursue correctly in the formative stages of litigation.

The risk otherwise is issuing against the wrong party, whether that be tortfeasor or insurer, and therefore having to make application to amend proceedings, substitute parties, or discontinue at a later date.

In determining the Pre-Action Disclosure Application, the court will have regard to whether or not the information being requested will assist in the dispute being resolved[12].

In ***Rose v Lynx Express Ltd***[13], the Court of Appeal held:

> "… courts should be hesitant, in the context of an application for pre-action disclosure, about embarking upon any determination of substantive issues in the case. In our view it will normally be sufficient to found an application under CPR r.31.16(3) for the substantive claim pursued in the proceedings to be properly arguable and to have a real prospect of success, and it will normally be appropriate to approach the conditions in CPR r.31.16(3) on that basis."[14]

In terms of Pre-Action Disclosure Applications a Claimant may opt to make prior to the commencement of proceedings might include:

- Applications for details of the fault driver's insurer in contract under the "driving other cars" extension.

---

12 Civil Procedure Rule 31.16(3)(d)

13 [2004] EWCA Civ 447; [2004] 1 B.C.L.C. 455

14 Editorial note 31.16.5 of the White Book [2023]

- Applications for the identity of the driver of the fault vehicle in cases where the driver was unidentified or untraced.

- Applications for an address for service of the fault driver (this being a relevant requirement where indemnity is withdrawn and the fault driver is required to be a party so a valid Judgment can be obtained against them pursuant to s.151 RTA 1988).

The costs regime is fairly stringent in Pre-Action Disclosure Applications and the general rule is that the Applicant will pay the Respondent's costs of the application[15] however the court does, and often will, utilise its discretion to make a different order having regard to "all the circumstances of the case" such as the reasonableness of the application generally, including a party's failure to comply with a request and / or delay on their part.

The need to identify the fault driver of a vehicle has now been placed into sharp focus following the Supreme Court's decision in the case of **Cameron v Hussain**[16], which forms the subject matter of the next chapter of this book.

15 Civil Procedure Rule 46.1

16 [2019] UKSC 6

CHAPTER EIGHT

CAMERON V HUSSAIN [2019] UKSC6 & DRIVERS UNIDENTIFIED

The Supreme Court's ruling in the case of Cameron v Hussain re-affirmed important principles arising in respect of indemnity issues often encountered in claims arising from road traffic accidents, and also served to provide a degree of clarity in the context of claims involving unidentified drivers.

The law in this area was relatively settled until the Claimant was involved in accident in May 2013, sustaining injuries when her vehicle collided with a Nissan Micra. The driver of that Nissan Micra made off without stopping or reporting the accident to the police. The Claimant in that case argued that since they were able to identify the vehicle involved by reason of recording the vehicle registration mark, thereby being also able to identify the RTA Insurer as Liverpool Victoria Insurance Co (LV), then they should be able to properly pursue LV for their losses since LV had taken premiums in respect of the policy on account of the risk it was insuring against. That was an approach adopted as an alternative to the more commonly accepted practice of pursuing a claim with the Motor Insurers' Bureau in accordance with the Untraced Driver's Agreement.

In a decision which caused some disruption in the insurance arena, particularly of concern for insurer's, the Court of Appeal permitted the Claimant to do so and thereby allowed an application by the Claimant to pursue a claim against "the person unknown (driving the Nissan Micra)".

LV subsequently appealed to the Supreme Court and were supported by the Motor Insurers' Bureau as interveners (on account of the MIB sharing concerns that the liberty afforded to claimants to sue persons unknown could lead to an increase in fraudulent claims against insurers on account of the greater vetting and non-adversarial setting of the MIB's untraced driver scheme). The appeal was successful and it was re-established that Claimants could not pursue persons unknown and obtain Judgments which would subsequently require settling by the RTA insurer of the fault vehicle. To do otherwise would also preclude the insurer from pursuing a right of recovery under s.151(8) of the Road Traffic Act 1988 given the obvious difficulties in identifying the fault driver.

Lord Sumption had concerns with the lack of service, which was deemed integral to a fair and proper process, when he said

> *"It is a fundamental principle of justice that a person cannot be made subject to the jurisdiction of the court without having such notice of the proceedings as will enable him to be heard."*[17]

It was said that the Claimant's approach in the case "struck a procedural knot" since the provisions of the contingent liability pursuant to s.151 RTA 1988 were only engaged when a Judgment was obtained against the insured person. However, since no insured person could be identified, it was not possible to obtain a regular Judgment against such an individual in accordance with accepted procedure.

It was held that

> ***"In my view the appellant's characterisation of the grain of the legislation hits a very large knot: the obligation on insurers under section 151 arises when there is a judgment. To obtain a judgment a claimant must satisfy the requirements of both procedural and substantive law. As a general rule procedural law requires, as we have seen, that defendants in legal proceedings be named.***

17 Paragraph 17, ibid.

> *Indeed, the grain of the legislation, in my judgment, is that a defendant must be named. First, the insurer's right of recourse under section 151(8) will often be dependent, in practice, on a driver being identified. Even where identified drivers disappear, the insurer may have had the opportunity to obtain more details of an accident, and may also be able to trace them. With unnamed defendants that is very unlikely. Secondly, under the 1988 Act and its predecessors, it is the driver who must be insured, not the vehicle. That suggests that identity is important within the legislative framework."*[18]

In light of the findings of the Supreme Court it is now incumbent upon Claimants to fully establish the identity of the fault driver if they wish to engage the s.151 RTA liability since a Judgment against that person is required. Claimants and their representatives should therefore be advised to make all necessary enquiries with insurers, which may include a search of the Motor Insurer's Database and / or the making or relevant Pre-Action Disclosure Applications.

In the absence of such certainty, a Claimant should pursue a claim for losses against the Motor Insurers' Bureau under the Untraced Driver's Agreement, albeit the liability of the MIB to indemnify is limited as are the costs recoverable (see chapter 5).

[18] Paragraph 111 and 112, ibid.

CHAPTER NINE

IDENTIFYING THE CORRECT CAUSE OF ACTION

Once a claimant has successfully identified the party against whom they intend to prosecute a claim against, it is imperative that the correct cause of action is pursued. The failure to do so can have catastrophic consequences and in the worst case, may lead to the claim being struck out as disclosing no grounds for the cause of action[19].

The cause of action should be pleaded in accordance with Civil Procedure Rule 16 and set out in clear terms what, and against who, the cause of action is in the Particulars of Claim[20].

That may be a claim in negligence (against the wrongdoer) or in accordance with statute or regulations (as against the insurer or MIB).

The fault driver, his servant, or agent

In this situation the pleading would be one in straightforward negligence, setting out why the driver, his servant, or agent, were negligent in a series of particulars of negligence in the pleading. This cause of action requires no addition or inclusion of a defendant insurer since it proceeds solely against the individual in negligence.

---

19 Civil Procedure Rule 3.4(2)(a)

20 Paragraphs 4 and 6 of the Practice Direction 16 prescribe various mandatory information that must be included in claims for personal injury and credit hire respectively

The contractual insurer

When a claimant pursues a claim against an insurer in contract and the insurer has confirmed that indemnity is in place (meaning that the fault driver retains insurance coverage in accordance with the terms of his policy) then the Claimant is entitled to directly sue the insurer.

That entitlement to directly pursue the insurer as sole defendant is set out within Regulation 3 of the European Communities Regulations 2002, which provides as follows:

> *"(1) Paragraph (2) of this regulation applies where an entitled party has a cause of action against an insured person in tort or (as the case may be) delict, and that cause of action arises out of an accident.*
>
> *(2) Where this paragraph applies, the entitled party may, without prejudice to his right to issue proceedings against the insured person, issue proceedings against the insurer which issued the policy of insurance relating to the insured vehicle, and that insurer shall be directly liable to the entitled party to the extent that he is liable to the insured person."*

The Regulations therefore provide the Claimant with a cause of action to proceed against the insurer since the insurer will be directly liable to the Claimant to the full extent that they are liable to the insured person in contract. Provided that there are no issues with indemnity, a Claimant would be well advised to pursue the insurer as sole defendant and note that there is no need for a Judgment to be obtained against the fault driver since contractual indemnity remains intact. Note however that best practice should ordinarily dictate that both tortfeasor and relevant insurer are included as co-defendants to any claim in order to protect against any change in the indemnity position later, which would require amendment by way of application pursuant to Civil Procedure Rule 19 to add one of the parties later, thereby adding delay and expense to the litigation. However, where indemnity is confirmed, there is no need to include any party beyond that of the contractual insurer since the entitlement to directly pursue the insurer exists in accordance with Regulation 3.

The hybrid contractual insurer and s.151 Insurer

Whilst the status of these insurers may well differ in terms of their respective rankings on the indemnity tree of hierarchy, the method or grounds upon which a claim should be pursued against each is more or less identical.

In this situation, whether as an insurer in contract under the driving other cars extension, or as RTA Insurer of the vehicle on which the fault driver was not a named driver, both insurers will have withdrawn indemnity to the driver of the vehicle.

The insurers contingent liability (whether hybrid or RTA insurer) will therefore arise pursuant to s.151 of the RTA 1988. It will therefore be necessary to obtain a Judgment against the fault driver since the liability pursuant to s.151 is only to satisfy a Judgment so obtained against that driver.

Accordingly, claimants should issue against both fault driver and insurer for these purposes.

In doing so, the claimant will ensure compliance with s.151 RTA (since a Judgment will be obtained against the driver as First Defendant). The Particulars of Claim should also plead allegations of negligence in tort against the driver.

A secondary case should also be pleaded against the insurer, expressly relying upon the provisions of s.143 and 145 RTA 1988, referencing particularly that the insurer, as Second Defendant, had issued a policy of motor insurance (either to the First Defendant as insurer in contract, or in respect of the vehicle as RTA Insurer) in accordance with those rules.

The cause of action should then be pleaded on grounds of the insurer's contingent liability pursuant to s.151 RTA 1988 and their duty to satisfy any Judgment obtained against the driver of the vehicle.

In this case, it is not correct to pursue a direct cause of action against the insurer as there is no contractual indemnity in place, there can therefore be no liability directly to the fault driver from the insurer. That liability instead is provided through the mechanism of the statute.

The need to plead a primary case in negligence against the driver is therefore required in order to underpin the claim against the tortfeasor, since it is only by virtue of securing a Judgment against this individual that the s.151 RTA 1988 contingent liability will then arise as against the insurance company. The s.151 liability against the insurer is therefore needed to be pleaded as a secondary case in any Particulars of Claim when pursuing this cause of action.

CHAPTER TEN

THE CONSEQUENCES OF FAILING TO IDENTIFY THE CORRECT CAUSE OF ACTION

In the event that a Claimant does fail, or omit, to plead the correct cause of action against a Defendant insured, the Claimant will be faced with the need to make application to amend the statement of case to remedy the defective nature of the pleading. Alternatively, the claimant could find themselves on the receiving end of an application from the Defendant to strike out the claim pursuant to CPR 3.4(2)(a) as disclosing no grounds for the cause of action.

By way of reminder, the relevant rules vests a discretionary power within the court to strike out a statement of case

> **"... if it appears to the court—**
>
> (a) **that the statement of case discloses no reasonable grounds for bringing or defending the claim;"**[21]

Clearly, in the event that the Particulars of Claim pursue a cause of action wrong in law, such as pursuant to Regulation 3 of the European Community Regulations 2002 directly against an insurer which has withdrawn indemnity from the driver, then a Claimant cannot say the statement of case disclosed reasonable grounds and the court ought to be minded to strike the claim out.

---

[21] Civil Procedure Rule 3.4(2)(a)

A Claimant faced with this most undesirable scenario would however be well advised to consider drawing the court's attention to the case of *Soo Kim v Youg*[22]. The case acts as a persuasive authority to encourage the court, where it to find a statement of case is defective for demonstrating no reasonable grounds for the cause of action, to consider whether that defect is capable of remedy by amendment as opposed to the more draconian sanction of a strike out. The case lends assistance to Claimant's seeking the court's indulgence to at least be afforded the opportunity to amend the statement of case and can be found at editorial note 3.4.2[23] to CPR 3.4. Note however that in the example used to demonstrate the failure in the statement of case to address viable grounds for the cause of action, the remedy of reverting to a s.151 RTA pleading against the insurer would axiomatically call for an addition of the driver of the vehicle pursuant to CPR 19.4, which is why its simply best for Claimant's to get this right first time round. As will be explored below, the problem of amendment is aggravated when the primary limitation period has passed and the Claimant is in the invidious position of not only needing to substitute the cause of action, but a party too.

I recently attended a case in the Birmingham County Court, which encapsulates the risks faced by Claimants falling foul of this necessary requirement concisely.

In that case, the Claimant had brought a claim against the insurer only, predicated on the grounds of entitlement to pursue an insurer directly pursuant to Regulation 3 of the European Community (Rights Against Insurer) Regulations 2002. Unfortunately, for this particular claimant, the insurer in this case had reserved indemnity from the driver of the fault vehicle on grounds of non co-operation and failing to report the accident, in breach of the policy terms. Accordingly, there could be no direct cause of action against the insurer, since there was no "insured person" for the

---

22 [2011] EWHC 1781 (QB)

23 Pg 94 of the Civil Procedure Rules 2024 Volume 1

purposes of the regulations and the insurer owed no liability to him in its capacity as insurer in any event as the contract was no longer valid.

This information had been communicated to the Claimant and their representatives in the pre-issue stage and it was specifically mentioned that indemnity had been withdrawn.

Following the issue of proceedings and upon receipt of the Defence denying the claim on grounds that there was no cause of action, the proceedings being defective in failing to plead the correct cause of action, the claimant made application to a) amend the Particulars of Claim so as to be able to plead the correct cause of action against the insurer, which would be the contingent liability pursuant to s.151 RTA 1988, and b) to add the fault driver as an additional defendant.

The application failed and serves a warning to all claimants of the significant importance of getting the pleadings right first time around. The reason for its failure included a cross-application to strike out the claim per CPR 3.4(2)(a), which may have succeeded on its own merit, although the case was complicated further by the involvement of rules on limitation.

Limitation

The importance of pleading the correct cause of action is heightened in cases issued on the cusp of limitation.

The reason being that a more stringent test is applied to cases involving rules of limitation and requests to both add new parties to claims which have already passed the statutory limitation period and substitute new causes of action.

If a Claimant has pleaded the incorrect cause of action in a statement of case (such as pursing an insurer *only* as sole defendant pursuant to the EC Regulations when indemnity has in fact been withdrawn from the fault driver) and consequently needs to pursue an action pursuant to s.151 RTA 1988, it is apparent that the Claimant will need to add in the fault driver, since it is necessary to have a Judgment obtained against that individual which will then invoke the s.151 liability of the insurer to satisfy it.

The test to be applied for considering the adding or substituting of parties post-limitation however is one to be applied stringently by the courts. The relevant provisions can be found within Civil Procedure Rule 19.6(2):

> *"(2) The court may add or substitute a party only if –*
>
> *(a) the relevant limitation period was current when the proceedings were started; and*
>
> *(b) the addition or substitution is necessary."*

In determining whether or not the addition or substitution of a new party is "necessary" in accordance with the rule will be decided in accordance with Civil Procedure Rule 19.6(3):

> *"3) The addition or substitution of a party is necessary only if the court is satisfied that –*
>
> *(a) the new party is to be substituted for a party who was named in the claim form in mistake for the new party;*
>
> *(b) the claim cannot properly be carried on by or against the original party unless the new party is added or substituted as claimant or defendant; or*
>
> *(c) the original party has died or had a bankruptcy order made against them and their interest or liability has passed to the new party."*

As can be seen, the test of "necessary" is a rather narrow one, and the court will only look to grant such an application to add or substitute a new party in a very limited set of circumstances.

The first criterion of a party being named by mistake is unlikely to be engaged in similar applications to amend proceedings, since the decision to pursue an insurer only as a defendant is often a deliberate choice of the claimant or their solicitor, as opposed to some mistake or misnaming of a party.

Many defendants faced with such applications are likely to oppose the addition or substitution of a party on grounds that it is not necessary to add or substitute a party to dispose of the claim since it is axiomatic that any claim pleaded on an incorrect ground will likely fail by virtue of its own defect, and will therefore be "determined" albeit in a way adverse to the erring claimant.

Other applications a claimant may make, couched on grounds that the cause of action is wrong and needs to be amended, will also face something of an uphill struggle if made post-expiry of the limitation period.

The Court of Appeal provided guidance on the approach to be adopted by the courts to such applications in the case of ***Nemethi v Sabre Insurance***[24]. The claim involved that of passengers involved in single vehicle accident overseas in which the driver was fatally injured. The passengers issued claims against the insurer of the vehicle only pursuant to EC Regulations, entitling them a direct cause of action against the insurer. However, in that case the insurer owed no contractual indemnity to the driver of the vehicle when they were a deceased person and when the accident happened abroad. Accordingly, the claimants made applications to add the deceased's estate as a party to proceedings and also to amend the cause of action from that pleaded pursuant to EC

24 [2013] EWCA Civ 1555; [2014] C.P. Rep. 16:

Regulations, to obtain a Judgment against the deceased's estate and then look to enforce it pursuant to s.151 of the Road Traffic Act 1988. The applications were refused with reasons set out at editorial note 19.6.5 of the White Book setting out the findings of the Court of Appeal as follows:

> ***"The Court of Appeal held that** s.35 of the Limitation Act 1980 **did not empower the court to add or substitute the deceased's estate outside the limitation period in these circumstances. As to** r.19.6(3)(b), **the joinder was not necessary in order to maintain the original claim: it was sought in order to raise a new claim (in tort) against a new party in order to add to or replace the original claim (under statute) which had been brought against the original defendants. This was so even though both claims arose out of the same road accident and the original defendants were targeted as the ultimate payers under both of them. As to** r.19.6(3)(a), **the mistake that had been made as to the EU regulation was not a mistake which the court had power to remedy under** s.35 of the Limitation Act 1980: **the insurers had been made defendants as persons liable as insurers of the car, not because of any mistake made as to any liability they may have had as tortfeasors."***

In essence, that the Court of Appeal found in *Nemethi* was that the Claimants were not only attempting to substitute or add a new party to the litigation, but they were also attempting to substitute an entirely new cause of action. As the claimants in Nemethi found out, attempting to do so when limitation expired is likely to be viewed as too little, too late, and solicitors who make a similar mistake can likely be expected to cover the loss of claim on their own professional indemnity insurance.

A possible route to salvation does however exist via Civil Procedure Rule 19.6(4). In neither the case of Nemethi in the Court of Appeal, or in the failed application I attended in the Birmingham County Court, concerned an application by the claimants to extend the limitation period retrospectively. Any claimant seeking to amend their cause of action and

/ or add a new party post-expiry of limitation may therefore find that supplementing such applications with an application to extend limitation pursuant to CPR 19.6(4) may well bear fruit and avoid the problems encountered by the Nemethis. The rule in 19.6(4) affords the court a wide discretion in disapplying the statutory time limit for limitation and in that sense, provides a potential route out of the type of problems many claimants face when making applications to amend pleadings post-limitation.

The editorial note in the White Book at 19.6.7[25] encapsulates this very scenario in a nutshell, when it expresses:

> *"By way of example, consider a personal injury claim arising out of a road accident which is commenced within the time limit specified by s.11 and which names "X" as the defendant and correctly describes him as the owner of the vehicle allegedly driven carelessly. Assume that, after the expiry of the s.11 time limit the claimant seeks an order substituting the driver, "Y", as defendant. If that application is made under r.19.6(3)(a) it must fail; there is no mistake here as to the identity of X; the mistake here is as to whether X is liable in negligence. However, if the application is made under r.19.6(4) and is combined with an application under s.33, the court may, in its discretion, allow the substitution if, on the application under s.33, if "it directs that … section 11 … shall not apply to the claim … against the new party".*

In summary, whilst it is important to tread carefully with applications of the type mentioned in this chapter, the making of such does not necessarily spell the end of the claim when the gateway of 19.6(4) exists.

[25] Pg 558 of Civil Procedure 2024 Volume 1

I would recommend that readers consider the test laid down within section 33(3) of the Limitation Act 1980 and the case of *Hall v Ministry of Defence*[26] which are unfortunately, beyond the scope of this textbook.

[26] *[2013] EWHC 4092 (QB)*

PART THREE

INSURER'S AVOIDANCE OF INDEMNITY

CHAPTER ELEVEN

REPUDIATION & CANCELLATION OF POLICY AND SITUATIONS GIVING RISE TO AVOIDANCE

The insurer's decision to withdraw indemnity from its policyholder or insured driver will often rest on a number of considerations. The most obvious one is of course, a breach of the terms of the policy of insurance. It is significantly important that those acting for insurers are aware of their clients right to withdraw indemnity under the contract of insurance, and when it is engaged, since being vested within that knowledge could absolve an insurer completely of liability in the best-case scenario. Conversely, from a claimant's perspective, having an understanding of the insurer's right to avoid indemnity to them is fundamental to understanding what cause of action to choose and therefore, which path a claim should take, as explored in the preceding chapter.

It should be borne in mind that some of the rights insurers are entitled to exercise may give rise to an entitlement to withdrawing indemnity. But as we shall discover, such a right does not amount to an insurer being able to avoid liability to claimants or third parties altogether. Then there are other opportunities for the insurer to avoid indemnity altogether, and these will be so fundamental as to allow an avoidance of indemnity under a policy of motor insurance altogether – these are "absolute rights" of avoidance.

Before considering what the effects of a cancellation of policy means its worth firstly considering some of the situations in which such cancellation, or voiding of a policy, can arise.

Cancellation for misrepresentation or non-disclosure on inception

One of the most commonly encountered reasons an insurer will give for cancelling a motor policy of insurance will be a misrepresentation made by the insurer on inception of the policy. Such reasons for cancellation will sometimes be in respect of a failure by the insured person to disclose a motoring conviction (eg speeding offence), exaggerating the number of no claims discount, or misrepresenting the user of the vehicle and place it is normally kept (quite often this practice is referred to as "fronting" which is explored in greater detail later in this book).

In these situations, an insurer is entitled to cancel the policy of motor insurance and withdraw indemnity from its policyholder or insured driver. Whilst such misrepresentations would not necessarily entitle an insurer to avoid indemnity in respect of satisfying third party claims (per the contingent liability under s.151 RTA 1988) the effect of the withdrawal of indemnity would have ramifications for the cause of action and the insurer's rights of recovery against the insured in the event they end up satisfying a Judgment obtained against its insured driver.

Any insurer seeking to avoid for non-disclosure must show he was actually induced by the non-disclosure to enter into the policy on those terms (Pan Atlantic Insurance Co Limited v Pine Top Insurance Co Limited[27]).

Cancellation of policy for breach of a condition

Another reason giving rise to an insurer cancelling a policy of motor insurance or voidance of a policy will often be when a policyholder breaches a term of the insurance policy. This may be driving beyond the agreed annual mileage, driving the vehicle for a use not included within the policy (for example, commuting to work when the policy only entitles

---

27 [1995] AC 5001

use for social, domestic and pleasure usage). Whilst the definition of "use" shall be scrutinised in depth later in this chapter, for present purposes, as a breach of a warranty, term, or condition of the motor insurance policy, it is sufficient to justify cancellation of the policy or withdrawal of indemnity from the insured.

Other more obvious reasons giving rise to a cancellation would be a failure to pay the insurance premium, causing it to lapse, or not ensuring the vehicle has a valid MOT or road fund licence, for example.

CHAPTER TWELVE

THE EFFECT OF CANCELLATION UNDER S.152 RTA 1988 AND THE MOTOR VEHICLES (COMPULSORY INSURANCE) (MISCELLANEOUS AMENDMENTS) REGULATIONS 2019

The effect of an insurer cancelling an insurance policy is not always tantamount to them having no liability to satisfy a judgment obtained against a driver of the insured vehicle, unless they have successfully managed to effectively "downgrade" their status from s.151 RTA 1988 Insurer. It is thus important to distinguish between an insurer who simply cancels a policy of motor insurance and one which cancels the policy **and** has downgraded its status. The former leaves the insurer still with a contingent liability to settle claims of third parties (even if it can avoid having to pay its own insured anything) and preserves their rights of recovery against and insured, whereas the latter would allow an insurer to potentially avoid having to satisfy any Judgment arising out of the negligent usage of the vehicle at all following the downgrading.

When an insurer is however able to downgrade its status – effectively removing their contingent liability to satisfy a Judgment under s.151 RTA – then a claimant may have to look elsewhere to pursue a claim. The reason is that the removal of the s.151 RTA liability works so as to effectively remove the insurance policy coverage of the driver of the fault vehicle and the consequence is that the claim devolves to the MIB in accordance with the Uninsured Driver's Agreement.

The Motor Vehicles (Compulsory Insurance) (Miscellaneous Amendments) Regulations 2019

The effect of these regulations amended s.152 RTA 1988 to the extent that Insurance companies were no longer able to obtain a declaration to downgrade its status to that of an Article 75 insurer after an accident giving rise to a liability under the policy had taken place.

Prior to then, insurers could properly look at breaches of the insurance policy, which had taken place since its inception, or take into consideration misrepresentations that had been made on inception, in order to cancel the policy after an accident had taken place.

However following the implementation of the 2019 Regulations, only declarations obtained prior to 1st November 2019 are effective for the purposes of removing an insurers s.151 RTA 1988 liability.

That has led to an obvious downturn in the number of applications by insurers and those who represent them to downgrade status from s.151 RTA insurer to that of an Article 75 insurer, such are the narrow constraints of s.152 RTA 1988 following introduction of the 2019 Regulations.

Nowadays a motor insurer can only downgrade its status to Article 75 and obtain a s.152 declaration after 1st November 2019 if it is able to point to one of three exceptions, as follows:

i) "…before the happening of the event which was the cause of the death or bodily injury or damage to property giving rise to the liability, the policy … was cancelled by mutual consent or by virtue of any provision contained in it …"[28]

[28] S.152(1)(c) Road Traffic Act 1988

That is to say that the insurer and insured have mutually agreed to cancel the policy (most likely within the 14 day cooling off period when the insured has found a cheaper quote elsewhere, or the parties have agreed to cancel the policy for some other reason), or the insurer has cancelled in accordance with any provision within the policy (most commonly a failure to pay the premium or comply with some other condition by the insured eg. providing evidence of no claims discount).

ii) In accordance with s.152(2) RTA 1988, the insurer obtained a declaration <u>before</u> the accident on grounds of misrepresentation or non-disclosure as follows:

> <u>"No sum is payable by an insurer under section 151 of this Act in connection with any liability if, before the happening of the event which was the cause of the death or bodily injury or damage to property giving rise to the liability, the insurer has obtained a declaration</u>
>
> <u>(a) that, apart from any provision contained in the policy... , he is entitled to avoid the policy under either of the relevant insurance enactments ... on the ground that it was obtained—</u>
>
> <u>(i) by the non-disclosure of a material fact, or</u>
>
> <u>(ii) by a representation of fact which was false in some material particular, or</u>
>
> <u>(b) if he has avoided the policy under either of the relevant insurance enactments ...] on that ground, that he was</u>

> entitled so to do apart from any provision contained in the policy...[29]

iii) The use of the vehicle at the material time was not one provided by the policy to have been insured for. The entitlements of the insurer and status of vehicles and those persons driving them said not to have been insured for that usage at the material time is explored in more detail later in this chapter. For present purposes however, use for a non-insured purpose potentially gives rise to an insurer's entitlement to obtain a s.152 declaration and to downgrade its status to Article 75 insurer.

In the event that an insurer does not obtain a declaration to downgrade its status to Article 75 insurer, and thereby remove its s.151 RTA 1988 liability, then the effect of cancellation is of limited effect from a claimant's perspective since the liability to meet third party claim is still engaged. An insurer which cancels a policy of insurance but does not obtain such a declaration may only therefore avoid a liability to meet the claims of its own insured or policyholder. The other obvious benefit of cancelling a policy of motor insurance for insurers is that by doing so, they have preserved their right to seek a recovery of all damages and losses paid to third parties from the insured pursuant to s.151(8) of the RTA 1988.

The insurer who successfully obtains a declaration prior to the happening to the accident and / or in the event the usage is not an insured one, then immediate steps should be taken to remove itself from the Motor Insurance Database (MID) in order to avoid potential liability for claims occurring in the material period whilst that insurer remains on the MID (the effects of an insurer remaining as a named insurer on the MID at the material time of accident are considered in further detail later in this chapter).

29 S.152(2) ibid.

In light of the 2019 Regulations and how the reach of s.152 RTA 1988 has been limited in its scope so as to limit the avenues available to an insurer to downgrade its status "after the event" has happened, insurers would be well advised to carefully check its policies terms and conditions are sufficiently clear so as to justify a cancellation in accordance with s.152(1) RTA 1988 since the route to cancellation "by virtue of any provision contained in it (the policy" may not otherwise be available.

When a claimant is informed of cancellation of policies and withdrawal of indemnity from policyholders by defendant insurers then all due diligence in respect of the cause of action and precisely who to sue should be paid, as per the guidance given in Chapter 2.

CHAPTER THIRTEEN

S.148 RTA 1988 EXCEPTIONS AND THE "HYBRID CONTRACTUAL INSURER"

Having considered the effects of cancellation under s.152 RTA 1988 and the rather narrow set of circumstances such an application to downgrade is now available to a s.151 RTA Insurer, it is only appropriate to consider some of the avenues to cancellation that may be available to a s.148 RTA Insurer (or the "hybrid contractual insurer" as discussed in Chapter one).

Section 148 RTA 1988 sets out a number of possible routes to cancellation that are available to an insurer when considering whether or not to cancel a policy.

Those specific reasons for cancelling a policy pursuant to this statutory provision are helpfully set out in s.148(2) as follows:

(a) the age or physical or mental condition of persons driving the vehicle,

(b) the condition of the vehicle,

(c) the number of persons that the vehicle carries,

(d) the weight or physical characteristics of the goods that the vehicle carries,

(e) the time at which or the areas within which the vehicle is used,

(f) the horsepower or cylinder capacity or value of the vehicle,

(g) the carrying on the vehicle of any particular apparatus, or

(h) the carrying on the vehicle of any particular means of identification other than any means of identification required to be carried by or under [the Vehicle Excise and Registration Act 1994].

In the event that the driver of an insured vehicle was to breach any of the above exclusions to coverage, the "hybrid contractual insurer" would accordingly have ground to cancel the policy. The effect of the cancellation would be to a) withdrawn indemnity from the driver or policyholder under the policy, b) insulate the insurer from having to pay anything towards the driver or the insured vehicle's claim or loss, c) preserve rights of recovery against the driver of the insured vehicle or policyholder. It is significantly important however from a claimant's point of view, is that cancellation under one of these grounds would not absolve the insurer from a liability to meet any third-party claims. The reason for that overarching principle is that the insurer has not downgraded its status pursuant to s.151 RTA and therefore retains its contingent liability. The breach of policy for one of these reasons within s.148 RTA does not underpin an application to downgrade status or result in the removal of a s.151 liability.

For example, if a vehicle is declared to have five seats, but an irresponsible parent transports a number of their children and their friends to a football game or other children's activity, and there happens to be seven occupants in the vehicle, that breach of the policy would result in the insurer having an entitlement to cancel the policy under s.148 RTA 1988. It would not entitle an insurer to downgrade the status of s.151 RTA Insurer, in large part due to the constraints put in place by the 2019 regulations and the inability to downgrade post November 2019. The same would apply if the vehicle was modified so that it was of a greater horsepower or lesser weight, for example. These types of breach can therefore be deemed severe enough to result in a cancellation of the policy (depending upon the policy wording and terms) but minor enough so as to entitle an application by the insurer to downgrade. It would however preclude a claimant from pleading a direct cause of action pursuant to Regulation 3 of the European Community Regulations and instead require a cause of action predicated on the grounds of s.151 RTA 1988.

CHAPTER FOURTEEN

INSURED USE & EXCLUSIONS

As was discussed in Chapter twelve, one way an insurer could look to downgrade its status post November 2019 and downgrade its status from s.151 RTA 1988 Insurer would be to rely on the usage of the insured vehicle being one for which it was not insured at the material time.

This may hinge on not only the usage of the vehicle being not an insured usage, but also where about the vehicle is being used.

The most commonly insured usage of a motor vehicle is that of "social, domestic, and pleasure (SDP)" and provided that the usage of the vehicle was within that remit, subject to there being no other breaches of the policy or grounds for cancellation, the most obvious insurer would be the insurer in contract (before working down the tree of hierarchy as discuss in Chapter one). Other policies may also insure the use for business purposes, such as travelling in the vehicle for business or work (such as requiring use of the vehicle to carry out duties, for example, as a salesman or delivery driver, a taxi driver to carry fare paying passengers), or commuting to and from work.

The narrow scope of exceptions to coverage under s.151 RTA 1988 following the introduction of the *Motor Vehicles (Compulsory Insurance) (Miscellaneous Amendments) Regulations 2019* has naturally led more and more insurers to consider their rights when it comes to determining whether or not the use of the vehicle was one permitted within the policy of insurance. That has also led to a greater focus on the wording of policies, with many not only being specific as to what usage is insured (eg. SDP) but specifically prohibiting others (such as using the vehicle for racing, carriage of passengers for reward, delivery of goods, or for criminal enterprise).

The mechanism of the rules and legislation in this regard is perhaps best demonstrated by the case of *EUI v Bristol Alliance Ltd Partnership*[30]. The case concerned Mr James Williams, a man convicted of dangerous driving at speeds greater than 100mph in the outskirts of Bristol, causing grievous bodily harm to the Claimant and criminal damage to property including a House of Fraser store, incurring damage of more than two-hundred thousand pounds, whilst in control of the insured vehicle. The crux of the issue for the court to decide was whether or not the insurance policy covered liabilities for deliberately damaging property under section 145(3)(a) of RTA 1988. The court ruled that the policy did not extend that far so as to insure coverage of liabilities incurred as the result of using the vehicle to deliberately damage property since the terms of the policy expressly excluded any damage caused by the deliberate act of the driver. The Claimant was therefore unable to pursue the insurance company for their losses and was left to continue any action against the Motor Insurers' Bureau in accordance with the Uninsured Driver's Agreement. In addition, the court ruled that the exclusion of all subrogated claims was also effective.

The reasoning underpinning Lord Justice Ward in that case can be found in the wording of s.151 RTA 1988 itself canvassed as follows:

> "The liability of the appellant therefore depends upon the four preconditions set out in sections 151(1) and (2) being satisfied. As set out at [29] above, this depends on whether the defendant's liability **"is a liability covered by the terms of the policy … to which this certificate relates"** (emphasis added) as required by section 151(2)(a)."

In order to succeed in establishing a liability against the insurer pursuant to s.151 RTA 1988, the claimant therefore needs to establish that the use of the insured vehicle given rise to the loss was "a liability covered by the policy". That condition is underscored by s.143 RTA 1988 which

30 [2012] EWCA Civ 1267

prescribes "a person must not use a motor vehicle on a road [or other public place] unless there is in force in relation to the use of the vehicle by that person such a policy of insurance ... as complies with the requirements of this Part of this Act". That is important since s.143(1)(a) RTA 1988 allows a motor policy to be issued in compliance with s.145(3) RTA 1988 even when it specifically excludes cover for any liability that may be incurred. That rationale was adopted by Rix LJJ in *Charlton v Fisher*[31] (a case involving an accident on a private car park causing injury and damage) when it was held:

> *"That necessarily means that a policy can comply with the requirements of section 145(3) which does not insure a person or persons specified in the policy in respect of any liability which may be incurred, but only in respect of any liability which may be incurred whilst the **vehicle** is being used as permitted by the terms of the policy."*

It is important to understand why the policy's compliance with s.143 and s.145 RTA 1988 is engaged given that s.151(2)(a) RTA 1988 extends the insurer's contingent liability to "any matter where liability with respect to that matter is required to be covered by a policy of insurance under section 145 of this Act". That was in fact the Claimant's argument in the case of *EUI v Bristol Alliance Ltd Partnership* which was essentially that an insurer's liability is not just limited to the use actually insured by the policy, but to include liabilities which must actually be covered by the policy (so as to make it compliant with s.145RTA 1988).

Lord Justice Ward in *EUI v Bristol Alliance Ltd Partnership* deals with the point when he observed

> *"Clarification is given by section 151(2)(a). The liability must be "covered by the terms of the policy to which the certificate relates". Now we know what we are looking for. We are looking for the policy to which the certificate of insurance relates. A certificate of insurance*

31 [2002] QB 578

> *relating to that policy has to be delivered. Liability has to be covered by the terms of that policy."*[32]

Given that clarity on the extent of the liability of a policy issued in accordance with s.145 RTA 1988, a rather simplistic approach is arrived at when deciding what the extent of the insurer's liability is when it comes to usage of the insured vehicle, which is that it must be **"a liability covered by the terms of the policy ... to which this certificate relates".**

Therefore, if a particular use of the vehicle is not insured, or specifically excluded, then s.152(2)(a) is engaged in limiting the insurer's liability to indemnify a claim and pave the way for an application to downgrade to Article 75 insurer and that will apply to use by the insured driver, or those not driving the vehicle and not covered by the policy.

The case law is however not as clear when it comes to theft of the vehicle, since if a vehicle is stolen, and being driven by the alleged thief for social purposes, then technically it cannot be said that the vehicle was being driven for any use not insured by the policy (ie. the vehicle is still being used on the road for its intended use). In that sense, the insurer does not have an automatic right to downgrade its status to Article 75 insurer, and each case will need to be considered on its own merits. It must be noted that the case of *EUI v Bristol Alliance Ltd Partnership* concerned an admitted use of the vehicle for reasons it was not insured, such as deliberately driving the vehicle for with the intent of causing criminal damage or injury.

There are then other more obvious cases concerning interpretation of "use" within the meaning of the Road Traffic Act and causes of action which ought to be distinguished from having anything to do with usage. One such case is that of *Carroll v Taylor (& othrs)*[33] in which Mr Carroll unfortunately suffered catastrophic head injuries after being dropped off

32 Paragraph 50 [2012] EWCA Civ 1267

33 [2020] EWHC 153 (QB)

by a taxi driver in a suburb if Liverpool in the early hours of Sunday morning. Mr Carroll had asked to be dropped off at his home in Huyton, but rather than following the instructions of Mr Carroll, the taxi driver robbed him of his debit card and pin number by using a trick, before leaving Mr Carroll in another area of Liverpool of Old Swan. Whilst walking home, Mr Carroll fell over the barrier of a motorway bridge and was catastrophically injured. He brought a claim against the insurer of the taxi, QBE Insurance, on grounds that his injuries were caused "arising out of the use" of taxi which was required to be insured by the policy of motor insurance adopting the wording of s.145 RTA 1988.

In finding that the Claimant's injuries did not arise out of the use of the taxi, and in dismissing the claim, The Honourable Mrs Justice Tipples found "The facts of this case are very far removed from those of *Dunthorne v Bentley* and, in my view, are nowhere near the line for a successful claim against the taxi driver under section 145(3)(a) of the RTA."[34] Even if the injuries had been found to have arisen out of the use of the taxi vehicle, the Judge still found that the claim would have been dismissed in that case on grounds that the use for which the taxi driver was putting the vehicle – to steal debit cards from unwitting passengers – would not have been a use prescribed by s.145(3) and accordingly would have found that no liability existed pursuant to s.151(2)(a) RTA 1988.

There is however a need to approach cases engaging issues of insured use with a great degree of caution, exemplified none more so than by the tragic case of *Dunthorne v Bentley*[35] (which was specifically referred to in the case of Carroll by The Honourable Mrs Justice Tipples as "falling the right side of the line" when it comes to a Claimant establishing liability for a claim "arising out of the use of the vehicle").

---

34 Paragraph 83 (ibid).

35 [1996] RTR 428

In Dunthorne, Mrs Bentley had broken down in her vehicle and parked it at the side of the road with the hazard lights illuminating. She alighted that vehicle and stood around ten yards ahead of it as she called for assistance. Whilst stood at the side of the road, a colleague of Mrs Bentley's who had observed Mrs Bentley standing on the side of the road and accordingly brought her vehicle to a stop on the opposite side. The colleague engaged in a shouted conversation with Mrs Bentley through her car window whereupon Mrs Bentley ran out into the road only be knocked down and fatally killed by the vehicle being driven by Mr Dunthorne, who was injured in the accident whilst driving. In that case, it was held that Mrs Bentley had run into the road to seek assistance with the re-starting of her motor vehicle, and the act of doing so was accordingly "closely and causally connected with her use of the car". That decision was upheld by the Court of Appeal.

Any analysis of the use of the vehicle being insured or not will therefore call for a detailed analysis of the factual matrix of the case at hand. Anybody tasked with considering whether or not the use of the vehicle is likely to fall within the ambit of s.145(3) RTA 1988 would be well advised to consider the test set down in the case of *AXN v Worboys*[36], in which Sibler J summarised the principles of Dunthorne as follows:

> "First, that the concept of "arising out of" is a wider concept than "caused by"; secondly, that the focus of the inquiry has to be to consider whether the injuries of the claimant were matters "arising out of the use of the car"; and thirdly, that it is necessary to analyse the activities of the driver whose insurers are being sued to see what he was doing at the time when the injuries were suffered in order to ascertain if they were "arising out of the use of the car"[37].

Some other examples of "usage" in the context of injury and loss "arising out of the usage" of the insured vehicle concern "collecting and dropping

36 [2012] EWHC 1730 (QB)

37 Paragraph 38 (ibid.)

off" cases and are summarised at paragraphs 58 to 61 of the Judgment in *Carroll*.

Another case which lends assistance is that of Wastell v Woodward[38] in which Mr Woodward was the owner and operator of a hamburger van who routinely parked his van up at the side of the road for business, when he would place an advertisement sign across the street. On the occasion of the accident he left the van to cross the road and re-position the sign. As he was crossing back across the road he walked into the path of Mr Wastell's motorcycle and was fatally injured. Mr Wastell was also injured in the accident and successfully sued the estate of Mr Woodward for injury and loss. In finding that the accident arose out of Mr Woodward's use of the vehicle, Master Davison ruled that "temporally, geographically and qualitatively, the accident was closely linked to using the van on the road as a hamburger van" and found that Mr Wastell's claim against the insurer therefore succeeded.

I am sure by this point the inquisitive ones amongst you will be asking why then is an excepted use under the policy of insurance sufficient to give rise to a downgrading of the insurer's status, whilst one of those exclusions to coverage listed within s.148(2) RTA 1988 are not? The point was dealt with in *EUI v Bristol Alliance Ltd Partnership* when the subtle nuance between the two types of exclusion is dealt with by Lord Justice Ward at paragraph 42 of his Judgment, when it was said

> "Section 148 is interesting. It provides for the "Avoidance of certain exceptions to policies". Any attempt to restrict the insurance by reference to a number of matters listed in subsection 2 is of no effect. Those matters include the age or physical or mental condition of the persons driving the vehicle and that would include the physical state of the driver if he is the worse for drink. Once again the inference to be drawn from section 148 is that

38 [2017] 2 WLUK 717

whereas certain exceptions can be avoided, others will remain effective."

Finally, it would not be fair to end this chapter without some reference to the seminal case of R&S Pilling t/a Phoenix Engineering (Respondent) v UK Insurance Ltd[39]. The policy of insurance in that case confirmed, in most plain English, that the insured was covered "*if you have an accident in your vehicle and you kill or injure someone, you damage their property or you damage their vehicle*". The insured in that case was a garage and had permitted an employee to carry out repairs to his vehicle there. Whilst working on the car at the garage, the employee caused the car to be set on fire, leading to more than two million pounds worth of damage to the garage and neighbouring property. The insurer in that case issued an application seeking a declaration that it was not liable to cover the losses, which had been incurred by an employee working on his car on private land. The insured argued in the alternative that the repair had become necessary as a result of the car's usage on a road or other public place. At first instance, His Honour Judge Waksman granted the insurer's application on grounds that the employee's negligence did not amount to "use" of the car and that the fire had been caused as a result of his negligence whilst carrying out the repairs. The Court of Appeal overturned the decision at first instance on grounds that the wording of the policy was clear. However, the Supreme Court ruled that although the repair had arisen from that car's usage on a road or other public place, the insurance did not extend to the employee's negligent repair works, which was an independent cause of the fire and subsequent damage. The Supreme Court placed specific reliance on the wording of section 145 of RTA 1988, which mentioned not only the words "arising out of" but more significantly "caused by", which it found to be the operative words when interpreting what the insurance policy had covered. The "Phoenix case" therefore hinged on the specific wording of the policy and the need to read into the policy the wording of the Road Traffic Act so as to reflect the true intentions of the parties when it came to formation of the

[39] [2019] UKSC 16

insurance contract. Whilst each case will be decided on its own merits, it is vitally important that insurers pay the requisite attention to the specific wording in their policies, and to avoid the rather broad terminology as was utilised here. When considering "use" cases within the meaning of s.145 RTA 1988 one should therefore afford just as much weight to the words "caused by" as they do "arising out of" when determining if an exception to coverage is properly engaged.

"Use of the vehicle on a road or other public place"

Another route via which insurer's will often look to when downgrading their status under s.151 RTA 1988 is whether or not the insured vehicle was being used on public or private land.

Before delving into this area of the law in the context of insurance companies attempting to absolve themselves of an RTA liability to indemnify their policyholders for apparently driving the insured vehicle on private land, when the statute provides no duty to provide insurance for such usage, it is necessary to consider the intertwined nature of the concepts of EU Law and the Road Traffic Act 1988.

The difference between the typical model of motor insurance found in the EU when compared with that in the UK was initially discussed in Chapter one, which pointed out that EU countries tended to introduce policies of motor insurance covering vehicles and any driver of that vehicle, as opposed to the UK model, which so happens to issue policies to individual driver covering their usage of a specific vehicle (and sometimes others under DOC cover). The benefits of the EU model are that the arguments surrounding insurer status are simply non-existent, since the vehicle is either insured or it is not. In the UK a vehicle may be insured, subject to exclusions or exceptions, and may be covered by more than one insurer subject to how many individual so happen to have incepted a policy for that vehicle's usage or may be driving it under a DOC extension. This difference between the two systems of insurance is accentuated when one considers the use of the vehicle in the context of private or public land, since EU Directives and indeed case law, leans towards the EU model without consideration of the UK system, and thus rather problematically, the position of the Motor Insurers' Bureau.

By way of revision, a person "must not use a motor vehicle on a road or other public place unless the vehicle is insured" per Section 143 RTA 1988. The policy of insurance issued must also must persons "in respect of any liability which may be incurred by him or them in respect of the death of or bodily injury to any person or damage to property caused by, or arising out of, the use of the vehicle on **a road or other public place**"[40].

The position as canvassed within the Sixth EU Directive, Article 3(1) provides that "each Member State shall take all appropriate measures to ensure that civil liability in respect of the use of vehicles normally based in its territory is covered by insurance".

Historically, pre-Brexit, there was some confusion as to the reach of the EU Directive since it did not appear to cater for the limitation to insure for use "on a road or other public place", as was demonstrated by the interpretation and often inconsistent application of the leading case of ***Vnuk v Zavarovalnica Triglav (C-162/13).*** The Vnuk became something of the elephant in the room for Judges across the country since it was decided by the Court of Justice of the European Union in 2014. The case concerned a claim for damages by Mr Vnuk who was knocked off a ladder in a Slovenian farmyard by a trailer that was attached to a tractor, which was reversing across the yard. The CJEU in that case ruled that the use of the vehicle fell within its "normal function" and that when such use was found it mattered not whether that vehicle was on public or private land, provided such use was part of the normal function of the vehicle. The problems of that decision were very obvious, insofar as the mischief the Road Traffic Act sought to address was simply one of a road or other public place, whilst "normal function" appeared to bestow a wider definition to the one in the more narrower sense of use within the

40 Section 145(3) RTA 1988

RTA 1988. The concerns also stemmed as far as some commentators fearing an opening of the floodgates in respect of claims being brought arising from accidents with all manner of vehicle on private land, such as golf buggies, lawn mowers, and other electric vehicles, which may have otherwise required insurance. The Motor Insurers' Bureau was also left in the invidious position of accidents incurring a liability on private land not being insured within the terms of policies issued in the UK, moreover because they were not required to do so, pursuant to s.143 and s.145 RTA 1988.

In a move that was most gratefully received by all those operating in the motor insurance space in the UK, not least the Motor Insurers' Bureau, the government have since announced the removal of Vnuk from UK Law. The ruling had directed that the duty to insure extended to vehicles being used on private land, which was at odds with the RTA 1988 and as was acknowledged by the government when it removed Vnuk when the Motor Vehicles (Compulsory Insurance) Act 2022 received royal assent.

It remains to be seen what approach the court's will take to accidents on private land however given its previous approach to such incidents as confirmed by the decision in Lewis v Tindale[41] when the Claimant was run over on private land. In that case, it was held that the Motor Insurers' Bureau did owe a liability to satisfy the claim under the Uninsured Driver's Agreement as it was an emanation of the state in its capacity of the fund of last resort, and that it was the fault of the UK government for not properly implementing Article 3 of the Sixth EC Directive.

[41] [2019] 1 WLR 6298

CHAPTER FIFTEEN

ARTICLE 75 INSURER

Having paid consideration to the various avenues which are open to insurers for avoiding liability under the policy of insurance, and when that avenue can lead to an application to downgrading status from that of a s.151 RTA insurer, it is worth considering what the effects of such an application are.

The downgrading of status to Article 75 insurer can carry massive benefits for an insurer, not least because it moves them further down the branches of the tree of hierarchy as discussed in chapter one, and therefore potentially lead to another insurer picking up the tab for a claim. But moreover, it can often result in an insurer absolving itself from all liability of a third-party claimant whatsoever.

The result of a successful application for a declaration (which should be made via Part 8 claim form for declaratory relief), an insurer can avoid liability meaning any liability to meet the claim will devolve to the Motor Insurers' Bureau.

In practice, a Claimant often will still sue the named insurer but the mechanisms of the Motor Insurers' Bureau agreement with its members means that the insurer will only be acting as agent, with the ultimate liability to pay falling to the Motor Insurers' Bureau under the Motor Insurers' Bureau's Uninsured Driver's Agreement.

The effect of downgrading status to Article 75 insurer is that the insurer will no longer have to satisfy any Judgment arising out of the use of the vehicle. That means that the Motor Insurers' Bureau, or in the event there are multiple insurers, they will be projected in the list of priority for satisfying the Judgment. It also means that in a case of multiple tortfeasors (particularly useful in the case of passenger claims concerning multiple drivers) the other negligent driver (normally their contractual or s.151 insurer, or the MIB as the case may be) will be liable rather than the insurer. That also lends itself to the insurer having successfully downgraded being able to deploy the argument mandating that the claimant join another driver or insurer (as the case may be) pursuant to clause 14 of the Uninsured Driver's Agreement in order to argue for "meaningful degree" which the claimant may not have otherwise done but for the application to downgrade succeeding.

The application of this doctrine of Article 75 was recently placed into sharp focus in the case of Colley v Shuker[42] in which the Court of Appeal ruled that the Motor Insurers' Bureau should retain liability for settling the Judgment obtained by a passenger claimant involved in a road traffic accident, when the principle insurer had downgraded its status to Article 75 insurer, and the passenger knew that the driver of the vehicle was uninsured.

Mr Colley was able to obtain Judgment against Mr Shuker, but as he was unable to meet it, that Judgment fell to the motor insurer, only they had downgraded their status to Article 75 on the basis that the use of the vehicle by the son (who was not insured to drive the vehicle on his father's policy, or at all) was an excluded use. Mr Colley had initially argued that the downgrading of the insurer's status to Article 75 was in breach of the EU Directive, thought that was dismissed and the s.152 RTA 1988 exception was permitted. He then pursued the Motor Insurers' Bureau under Article 3 of the Sixth Motor Vehicle Insurer's Directive 2009. That was opposed by the Motor Insurers' Bureau on grounds that the vehicle had been insured initially and at the material time of the cause of action, and therefore the directive had been satisfied insofar as the requirements had been satisfied at the time. Freedman J found against the Motor Insurers' Bureau in deciding that it was obliged to satisfy judgments obtained by the innocent victims of road traffic accidents in situations whereby some other reason, even if insured initially, such as the workings

42 [2022] EWHC Civ 360

of national law, a vehicle would later become uninsured for the purposes of ensuring compensation is paid. This was a decision that follows the case of Lewis[43] and subject to some controversy given the claimant's knowledge that the driver carrying him in the car was uninsured. The litigation between the Motor Insurers' Bureau and the Secretary of State is continuing in this regard and will be likely be the subject of further change once a decision of the Court of Appeal or Supreme Court on the issue is handed down. However, for now, it can be established that if a vehicle is uninsured due to some incompatibility between EU and UK law, then the Motor Insurers' Bureau is likely going to be liable to meet the Judgment, in order to ensure that no innocent victim of a road traffic accident goes uncompensated.

43 [2019] 1 WLR 6298

CHAPTER SIXTEEN

S.152 RTA NOTICES

An important condition of the s.151 contingent liability arising, and oft overlooked, is that of the mandatory requirement to provide a s.152 notice to the insurer against whom the s.151 liability is being sought.

A party who pursues an action, which seeks to invoke the s.151(5) contingent liability of an insurer to satisfy a Judgment so obtained against the driver of their insured vehicle, is required to provide notice of their intention to do so pursuant to s.152(1)(a), which provides

> *"(1) No sum is payable by an insurer under section 151 of this Act—*
>
> *(a) in respect of any judgment unless, before or within seven days after the commencement of the proceedings in which the judgment was given, the insurer had notice of the bringing of the proceedings,"*

It follows therefore that any party failing to complying with this requirement to provide valid notice to an insurer pursuant to s.152 cannot subsequently pursue an action against the insurer on these grounds since the insurer's liability comes to an end by reason of that failure. It must be noted that the requirement for providing such a notice is only required if a party intends to pursue a cause of action based on s.151 and is not necessary if pursuing an insurer for recovery of compensation for example, on the basis of the EC (Rights Against Insurers) Regulations 2002.

A failure to comply with this provision would accordingly give rise to a very obvious defence becoming available to an insurer, seeking to escape a contingent liability pursuant to section 151. Claimants should also note that the requirement to give notice must be adhered to when issuing proceedings against the driver of the vehicle against who they intend to obtain a Judgment the insurer would subsequently be required to satisfy. Of course it would be best practice however to insure that a valid notice is given to the insurer of the vehicle in all situations, even if one does not intend to pursue a s.151 liability and even if indemnity is confirmed and a direct cause of action arises under the Regulations or in negligence, since the indemnity position is often subject to change.

The effect of s.152 is therefore to limit the scope of s.151 if no proper notice is served because the insurer liability comes to an end. The purpose of the legislation appears to be to be to offer form of protection to insurers who may otherwise have taken steps to protect its position when facing the possibility of a judgment against its insured that it would later be on the hook to satisfy (such as cancelling the policy, withdrawing indemnity, or seeking a declaration). Obviously, without notice, insurers would be left carrying the can of satisfying a Judgment obtained out of proceedings they knew nothing about.

There is a paucity of case law in the area of "s.152 Notices" and what would constitute the service of valid notice. Some Insurers may even look to argue that a valid notice has not been served unless that was done in writing and specifically referencing the relevant statutory provision. However, a consideration of some cases that have come before the courts on this point suggest that would be setting too high a bar for Claimants to satisfy the requirement.

The issue was explored by the Court of Appeal in **Nawaz.v.Crowe Insurance**[44] in respect of firstly, whether or not notice was given to "an appropriate person", and secondly, whether such notice was sufficient to satisfy the rule.

Mr Nawaz was the driver of a vehicle, in which Mr Hussain was a passenger, and which was involved in a car accident with another vehicle being driven by Mr Chaudry. Proceedings were issued against Mr

44 [2003] EWCA Civ 316

Chaudhry by Mr Nawaz and Mr Hussain and a Judgment in default was subsequently obtained. Mr Nawaz pursued the insurers of the vehicle being driven by Mr Chaudry, Crowe Insurance, pursuant to s.151(5). The insurer argued that they had not been served with the requisite s.152 notice and so owed no liability to satisfy the default judgment.

The issue of notice in Nawaz arose out of a telephone conversation between a Trainee Solicitor of the Law Firm representing Mr Nawaz and Mr Hussain, and a Legal Secretary to the Partner of a Law Firm instructed to represent the insurer. During the course of conversation the Trainee Solicitor had asked the Legal Secretary for the address of the Defendant in view of proceedings about to be issued but was told that information could not be given out. The Legal Secretary in question failed to tell the Partner about the contents of that telephone conversation. Even though s.152 RTA was not specifically mentioned by the Trainee Solicitor, the Court of Appeal upheld the District Judge's decision at first instance that

> "That conversation is quite clear notice that proceedings are to be commenced and, indeed, proceedings were subsequently brought within a matter of three weeks or so, so it was clearly those proceedings which were referred...What she has to have done is to have communicated that she was intending to bring those proceedings and I am satisfied that that call did take place."[45]

It is important to note that the Trainee Solicitor in the Nawaz case had not event appreciated the need to give a s.152 Notice, had not referred to that provision in the conversation, but moreover, that the Legal Secretary was also an appropriate person to who notice could be given notwithstanding that the Secretary had no authority to receive communications of this sort.

---

[45] Paragraph 14 (ibid.)

The decision in Nawaz appears to follow the guidance of Lord Justice Kennedy in the case of Desouza v Waterlow[46] when he says

> "There may well be other cases in which contact, even an informal contact, shortly before the commencement of proceedings would put the insurer in the position of having notice of the bringing of the proceedings -- everything would depend on the facts of the case, but a prudent solicitor would be well advised to ensure that the insurer received written notice within 7 days after the commencement of proceedings. There can then be no room for argument."

As it so happened, the insurer was still entitled to set aside the Judgment in Nawaz on grounds of suspected fraud, but the ruling in Nawaz on appropriate persons to accept a notice, as well as the sufficiency of a s.152 Notice sets a very low bar for Claimants to satisfy that a valid s.152 Notice has indeed been served on an insurer.

It is worth adding here that such is the make up of first notification claims nowadays, whether initiated on the MOJ or Official Injury Claims Portals, taken with the existence of the Motor Insurers' database, there really should be no excuse for not giving insurers the requisite notice of a claim.

However, the case law appears to support that the notice need not be in writing and can in fact be given orally by a party. That would then leave the timeframe as the critical component of the rule to comply with, requiring notice seven days either side of the issuing of proceedings.

Notwithstanding the findings in Nawaz, and those cases cited coming before it, practitioners would do well to remember that there can be no substitute for a notice in writing, prior to the expiry of the deadline for giving such a notice and making clear that notice is being provided

46 [1999] RTR 71

pursuant to s.152RTA. Taking that step would obviously eliminate any risk of a defendant seeking to raise invalid notice as a defence later. Every case will of course turn on its own factual matrix and as a warning shot to all those acting for claimants, I ought to remind you of the further guidance given by Lord Justice Kennedy in De Souza as follows[47]:

(1) To show that the insured had notice of the bringing of the proceedings there must be more than evidence of a casual comment to someone who at times acted as an agent for the insurers (see Herbert v RPA Company).

(2) Any notification relied upon must not be subject to a condition which may or may not be fulfilled (see Weldrick and Harrington) but if the only condition is one which requires action from the recipients which they choose not to take then by making that choice they render the notice unconditional and thus effective (see Ceylon Motor Insurance Association Ltd).

(3) The notice can be oral, and it need not even emanate from the claimant (see Harrington and Desouza). It can be given before proceedings have commenced, and it need not be specific as to the nature of the proceedings, (Desouza) or the court (see Ceylon and Harrington).

(4) Whether in any given case it is shown that the insurer had notice of the beginning of the proceedings (as opposed to the making of a claim) is a matter of fact and degree (Desouza).

47 Para 8 [2003] EWCA Civ 316

PART FOUR

RECOVERY ACTIONS

CHAPTER SEVENTEEN

THE INSURER'S RIGHTS OF RECOVERY

When an insurer cancels or voids a policy of motor insurance, but falls short of downgrading their status to that of an Article 75 insurer, the s151 RTA contingent liability remains albeit the insurer shall retain its rights of recovery under that section as against its policyholder or driver of the insured vehicle.

This will be the case when an insurer has cancelled a policy for either misrepresentation on inception, or non-disclosure, but failed to obtain the declaration to downgrade their status prior to the event happening (unless done prior to 1st November 2019 per the Motor Vehicles (Compulsory Insurance) Regulations of 2019). Another example where this situation would arise might be if one of the exclusions to coverage under s.148(2) applies (see Chapter 13), which would permit an insurer to withdraw indemnity from a policyholder but not entitle them to avoid liability to meet a Judgment. Other common examples would be where the policyholder has breached some other condition of the policy but the insurer has chosen not to, or failed, to obtain a declaration.

The contingent liability to satisfy a Judgment obtained against the driver of the insured vehicle, even when the policy of insurance restricts that liability (ie. if the policy is cancelled) is set out within s.151(5) RTA 1988 as follows:

> *"Notwithstanding that the insurer may be entitled to avoid or cancel, or may have avoided or cancelled, the policy... , he must, subject to the provisions of this section, pay to the persons entitled to the benefit of the judgment—*

(a) as regards liability in respect of death or bodily injury, any sum payable under the judgment in respect of the liability, together with any sum which, by virtue of any enactment relating to interest on judgments, is payable in respect of interest on that sum,

(b) as regards liability in respect of damage to property, any sum required to be paid under subsection (6) below, and

(c) any amount payable in respect of costs."

The right of recovery of an insurer can be found within s.151 RTA 1988 in the following two situations:

Firstly, where the insurer owes a contingent liability to satisfy a Judgment obtained against a person insured under the policy of insurance, even if the insurer had cancelled, or was entitled to cancel the policy:

"(7) Where an insurer becomes liable under this section to pay an amount in respect of a liability of a person who is insured by a policy [...], he is entitled to recover from that person—

(a) that amount, in a case where he became liable to pay it by virtue only of subsection (3) above, or

(b) in a case where that amount exceeds the amount for which he would, apart from the provisions of this section, be liable under the policy [...] in respect of that liability, the excess."

And secondly, in respect of persons not named on the policy of insurance (often uninsured drivers who were driving the vehicle at the material time) as follows:

Where an insurer becomes liable under this section to pay an amount in respect of a liability of a person who is not insured by a policy... , he is entitled to recover the amount from that person or from any person who—

> *(a) is insured by the policy... by the terms of which the liability would be covered if the policy insured all persons... , and*
>
> *(b) caused or permitted the use of the vehicle which gave rise to the liability."*

Section 151(7) and 151(8) therefore operate so as to allow the insurer a "safety net" of knowing that even though they owe a contingent liability to settle third party claims, notwithstanding that the insured or driver of the vehicle, has breached some term of the policy, that they have a right of recovery for their losses as against the insured or driver at the material time.

The critically important feature of s.151 rights of recovery is that the insurer must ensure that a Judgment is obtained against the negligent driver of the vehicle. That is because s.151 operates so as to only allow a recovery of sums paid under a contingent liability to satisfy a Judgment.

A failure to adhere to this compulsory requirement will likely result in a claim being struck out or dismissed at trial.

The obvious reason for this is to ensure fairness and transparency of the Judgment paid. If for instance, the debt was paid following acceptance or making of an offer, the court adjudicating upon the recovery action could not be sure that the sum paid was a reasonable one and would have to essentially hold a mini-trial of the quantum of all the losses paid for in the primary action as against the driver / insured, which the court will not entertain.

As a matter of best practice therefore, before settling any claim arising out of the use of the insured vehicle giving rise to third party claims, the insurer and those representing them must ensure that the claim is litigated and that a Judgment is entered against the driver of the insured vehicle.

Many insurers and their solicitors will no doubt point to the economics of such an approach, however a failure to do so will mean that the requirements of s.151 RTA are not capable of being met, and with that the rights of recovery will die also.

Of course, the merits of a recovery action should always be a deciding factor. If the party subject of any recovery action is of no assets and a "man of straw" well then clearly there should be no appetite for allowing the claim against the tortfeasor to become litigated, if the recovery action is never likely to be pursued. Likewise, if the economics of settling the claim pre-issue on best possible terms for the insurer, outweigh the benefits of allowing the claim to be issued to preserve a recovery action, then there would be no point in not engaging in mediation at the earliest opportunity without needing a Judgment to be entered before settlement.

In any case, whenever a recovery action is contemplated or intended to be pursued, it can only be done under s.151 RTA when a Judgment is obtained against the driver of the insured vehicle, since the obligation to satisfy the Judgment on a contingent liability is precisely that, one of satisfying "a Judgment".

Once proceedings have been issued it is imperative therefore that the driver of the insured vehicle is included as a party to the claim. For instance, if the proceedings are issued directly against the insurer (which would be wrong in the first place since the only direct cause of action accrues under Regulation 3 of the EC Regulations 2002), the claimant should be invited to amend the particulars to plead a s.151 cause of action and to join the negligent driver as a Second Defendant.

Alternatively, if proceedings have been issued solely against the tortfeasor in negligence, it will be necessary to make an application pursuant to Civil Procedure Rule 19.4 to join the insurer into proceedings as a Second Defendant. Such applications are often made by solicitors for the defendant insurer on grounds that they retain a financial interest in the outcome of the proceedings and have a contingent liability to satisfy any

Judgment so obtained against the First Defendant driver. Lord Denning MR set out the principle for this rationale in the case of **Gurner v Circuit**[48] as follows (even though he was referring to the Motor Insurers' Bureau, the principle still holds true for defendant insurers):

> "It seems to me that when two parties are in dispute in an action at law, and the determination of that dispute will directly affect a third person in his legal rights or in his pocket, in that he will be bound to foot the bill, then the court in its discretion may allow him to be added as a party on such terms as it thinks fit.
>
> It is thus apparent that the Motor Insurers' Bureau are vitally concerned in the outcome of the action. They are directly affected, not only in their legal rights, but also in their pocket. They ought to be allowed to come in as defendants. It would be most unjust if they were bound to stand idly by watching the plaintiff get judgment against the defendant without saying a word when they are the people who have to foot the bill".

If acting for Defendant insurance in this scenario, practitioners should also be aware of the occasional need to sometime accompany any application to join with an application to set aside any Judgment in default (in the situation where there are other concerns prevalent in the case beyond those of indemnity)

48 [1968] 2 (QB) 587

CHAPTER EIGHTEEN

DEFENCES

Once a claim is issued, or indeed threatened by an insurer, against an insured or driver of the insured vehicle, that is of course by no means a closed book. The insurer seeking a recovery in line with its entitlement under s.151 RTA will still need to prove its claim and this chapter is designed to look at some of the defences that might be available to a person sued under this statutory provision.

"Judgment?"

The first and perhaps most obvious defence, is that of the need for a Judgment to have been obtained. So if for instance, the insurer has settled the claims against the driver of the insured vehicle without a Judgment having been obtained against that party, then s.151 RTA rights of recovery are of no effect.

"Insurer?"

Another potential technical defence of the claim may arise for the defendant in a recovery action if it can be established that the claimant (insurer) is not in fact an insurer within the meaning of the Road Traffic Act 1988. The s.151 RTA right is only reserved to "insurers" and it can sometimes be the case that claims are incorrectly pursued in the name of managing agents, subsidiaries, or trading styles of insured companies, which should always be the insurer with the right and powers to effect and issue policies of motor insurance in the UK pursuant to s.145 RTA 1988, which is most likely the entity named on the insurance certificate. Any other entity will normally not hold the requisite locus standi to bring a s.151(7) or (8) right of recovery.

The Consumer Insurance (Disclosure and Representations) Act 2012

Another defence, which an individual made the subject of a s.151 RTA recovery action could deploy, is found within The Consumer Insurance (Disclosure and Representations) Act 2012 ("CIDRA 2012"). If the insurer in a recovery action is asserting rights of cancellation on grounds of any purported misrepresentation, the insurer would need to show that they would not have entered into the contract of insurance on any terms having knowledge of that misrepresentation, would have entered into the insurance contract on different terms, or would have entered into the insurance contract but would have charged a higher premium. This is otherwise known as "the inducement test" as canvassed within Pan Atlantic Insurance Co Limited v Pine Top Insurance Co Limited when Lord Mustill said that the words "*influence the judgment of a prudent insurer*" "*denotes an effect on the thought process of the insurer in weighing up the risk*". There is also no presumption of inducement even where it was proven that the non-disclosure or misrepresentation was material per *Assicurazioni Generali v ARIG*[49]. When such defences are engaged, evidence of the insurer's underwriter will often be determinative, and without such evidence an insurer will likely struggle to prove that they would not have undertaken the risk. So even, when a recovery action is predicated on a material non-disclosure or misrepresentation, it is by no means the end of the matter and the insurer should still be put to proof in respect of inducement.

The Insurance Act 2015

The defendant in a recovery action would also be well advised to consider the provisions of the Insurance Act 2015.

49 [2003] Lloyd's Rep IR 13

An otherwise insured person who has had indemnity withdrawn from them may otherwise be able to rely on the provisions of section 11 of the 2015 Act as follows:

> "If a loss occurs, and the term has not been complied with, the insurer may not rely on the non-compliance to exclude, limit or discharge its liability under the contract for the loss if the insured satisfies subsection (3)."

In that context, an insurer will not be able to rely on withdrawing indemnity and seek rights of recovery if the non-compliance with the policy did not directly cause the loss (ie. driving over the declared mileage at the point of inception of the policy during the course of the contract of insurance, or not declaring a motoring conviction) if that misrepresentation did not directly cause the loss incurred under the policy. That defence will only be available however where the insured is able to prove their compliance with section 3 of the Insurance Act 2015 to the extent that <u>"Before a contract of insurance is entered into, the insured must make to the insurer a fair presentation of the risk."</u> The interpretation of what constitutes a "fair presentation of the risk" remains open to debate and is yet to be subject to any determination in higher court jurisprudence. Further guidance as to how an insured may be able to demonstrate compliance is however available within section 4 of the 2015 Act.

A defendant in recovery proceedings may also look to lean upon the guidance provided in the Insurance Distribution Directive (EU) 2016/97 pursuant to article 17(1) and rule 2.5 of the Insurance Code of Conduct Business Sourcebook requiring insurers to act honestly, fairly and professionally in the best interests of the insured as a consumer.

CHAPTER NINETEEN

CLAIMS FOR EXEMPLARY DAMAGES

The insurer's claims for recovery are often supplemented by claims for exemplary damages where it can be proven that the insured acted fraudulently or neglectfully on inception of a policy or pursuit of a claim against their insurer. The right of recovery will often not require any s.151 entitlement but will be founded upon a pleading of breach of contract and tort of deceit, where for example, the insured has misled the insurer in respect of their own claim under a policy.

In the context of a motor claim, that might arise in a situation where the insured claims for damage in respect of their own vehicle that was pre-existing or caused by their own fault.

In these cases engineering evidence will often be crucial in discrediting the insured's version of events and the policy should be repudiated. The claim for recovery of all costs and outlay paid in respect of dealing with the insured's claim against their own policy should plead particulars of deceit, breach of contract, and if necessary, consider raising a claim for exemplary damages pursuant to Rookes v Barnard[50].

When an insurer pursues a claim for exemplary damages it should bear in mind the need to deter insurance fraud and specifically encourage the court to act on grounds of public policy in making any such orders sufficiently proportionate to act as a deterrent. Simply repaying the debt incurred by the insurer with costs is more often than not inadequate as a deterrent.

---

50 [196AC 1129

PART FIVE

FRAUDULENTLY INCEPTED POLICIES AND SOLD VEHICLES

CHAPTER TWENTY

FRAUDULENTLY INCEPTED POLICIES

When issues of indemnity are engaged in any motor claim, the occurrence of insurance fraud can unfortunately be increased. That is not to say that because indemnity is withdrawn or a policy has been cancelled by the insurer, it must lend itself to an assumption fraud is in play – quite the contrary. However, one reason an insurer may often look to withdraw indemnity under a policy of motor insurance might be owing to a reason or explanation that emanates from fraud, such as the non-cooperation of an insured. Why else would a party involved in litigation not seek to absolve themselves of responsibility and assist their own case?

The most common examples of this type of fraud include "fronting" of insurance policies – a situation used to describe a policy taken out for a genuine vehicle and for a genuine usage, but that uses the details of an invented person or someone more senior to the actual user of the vehicle to obtain lower insurance premiums (either by using an address which would attract a lower premium by reason of it being situate in a lower crime area for example, or the details of a person who is older or in a certain profession for the same purpose). Of course, obtaining insurance under this guise is illegal and in contravention of the Fraud Act 2006, potentially falling within category 5 harm fraud.

Another type of insurance fraud falling into this category would also be the practice of "Ghost broking", which typically involves individuals or entities posing as legitimate groups of insurers or intermediaries promising inception of motor policies for much cheaper insurance premiums than those which are readily available in the consumer market. The practice involves the "Ghost broker" providing potentially false details to the primary insurer and / or falsifying documents. Quite often the insurance premium will not have even be paid to the insurer causing the policy to lapse.

Whenever an insurer is able to establish foul play and detect that a policy of motor insurance has been incepted fraudulently, the policy should be cancelled and voided *ab initio* (back to inception). Such vehicles of insurance can sometimes be used as part of a wider scheme of insurance fraud to stage or induce accidents giving rise to motor claims, although that subject does not form part of the subject matter of this textbook.

In the event that a claim has been made against the policy in a situation where the policy was incepted on a fraudulent basis, the insurer should look to deny the claim and if necessary, raise the defence of ex turpi non causa in denying any claim the insured pursues.

CHAPTER TWENTY-ONE

SOLD VEHICLES & THE OPERATION OF THE MOTOR INSURER'S DATABASE

A common technical issue often arising in the scope of motor indemnity claims can involve the situation of who is liable to meet the claim if the vehicle has been sold before the accident but the insurer prior to the sale remains on the Motor Insurer's database ("MID")?

This scenario often creates confusion and is often contentious when it comes to deciding whether or not the insurer named on the MID remains liable for any Judgment arising out of the use of the insured vehicle pursuant to section 151 RTA 1988.

The reported case of Nagorski -v- Nikolics & Tradewise Insurance Company Limited (Liverpool County Court, 2021) whilst not a binding authority is a persuasive authority in support of the reasoning as to why the entry of an insurer on the MID is not proof of insurance.

The case concerned a road traffic accident in which Mr Nagorski, driving a Toyota motor car was involved in a collision with a Vauxhall Zafira, being driven by Mr Nikolics on 26 September 2018. A search of the MID revealed that Tradewise Insurance had issued a policy of insurance in respect of the Vauxhall to Mr Tibor Kiss t/a tibor Autos notwithstanding that evidence procured from the DVLA indicated that the Vauxhall had been transferred from Mr Kiss to Mr Nikolics on 6th August 2018, one month and twenty days prior to the accident. Nonetheless, the Vauxhall remained insured according to the MID as at the date of the accident. Mr Nagorski argued that Tradewise were liable to meet his claim since they were the relevant insurer named on the MID and that essentially, their obligations did not cease on the sale or disposal of the vehicle whilst the policy had not been cancelled. Recorder Parrington found against Mr Nagorski and ruled that the presence of an insurer on the MID did not bind them. The Judge in that case relied on the policy of wording requiring that the Vauxhall, or insured vehicle on the trade policy, be within "the custody or control" of Mr Kiss "for motor trade purpose". Placing reliance on Williams v Bristol Alliance and the interpretation of s.152(a) and (b) RTA 1988, it could not be said that the policy provided an indemnity in respect of Mr Nikolics use once the vehicle had been sold to him.

Perhaps a more emphatic demonstration of the sale of a vehicle effectively bringing to an end any insurable interest in the vehicle is however found in the case of **Tattersall v Drysdale**[51], which was not relied upon in the case of Nagorski. The case of Tattersall remains good law in respect of insurer's liability expiring upon the sale, and surrendering of possession, of a motor vehicle insured by the vendor.

There is however a note of caution to be exercised when considering whether a policy of motor insurance extends coverage beyond the sale of the vehicle when it comes to considering a case involving driving other cars ("DOC") extensions. In the case of **Dodson v Peter H. Dodson Insurance Services**[52] Lord Justice Mance carefully considered the wording of a policy of insurance permitting Mr Dodson to drive other vehicles under a policy of insurance in respect of a vehicle he had sold, when deciding that coverage did extend beyond the period of his ownership of the vehicle for which the policy was issued, and that the insurer did owe him an indemnity in respect of third party claims for his negligent driving of another person's car under the DOC extension. This case serves as a timely reminder that the wording of policies is significantly important. Mr Dodson had incepted a policy of motor insurance in respect of his own motor vehicle which afforded him a driving other car extension, and after selling that vehicle, he was involved

[51] [1935] 2 (KB) 174

[52] [2001] 1 Lloyd's Rep. 520

in an accident whilst driving his mother's car with her consent. His own insurers contended that the policy had lapsed on the sale of his own vehicle and declined indemnity on the basis that he had not sourced his own replacement vehicle. His mother's insurer accepted their contingent liability pursuant to s.151 RTA but sought to recover their outlay from Mr Dodson, who in turn, brought an action seeking an indemnity from his parent's insurance brokerage firm who had issued him with his policy on grounds of negligent advice. Lord Justice Mance however found that the policy of insurance granting him a driving other car extension continued to be valid in terms of providing an indemnity beyond the sale of his own car and for the entire duration of the policy as it was not specific as to when he was required to have replaced his car.

Whilst the Dodson case serves as a warning to insurers, particularly those providing DOC extensions, it would be best advice to ensure that the MID is always kept up to date and that insurers do not leave the keeping to the database to their insureds. This is especially important when considering downgrading to Article 75, since evidence of cancellation on the MID would ordinarily be required to be shown prior to any application having been made.

However it must be borne in mind that there is a paucity of higher court jurisprudence in this area and until the courts provide some more guidance it remains to be seen how such issues will continue to develop in practice.

MORE BOOKS BY LAW BRIEF PUBLISHING

A selection of our other titles available now:-

'A Practical Guide to Probation Breaches and Other Applications' by Mark Thomas
'A Practical Guide to Remarriage and Divorce' by Cordelia Williams & Claire Howard
'A Practical Guide to Privacy, Transparency, Reporting Restrictions and Closed Proceedings in the Court of Protection' by Laura Mannering
'Beaumont on Barristers – A Guide to Defending Disciplinary Proceedings (Second Edition)' by Marc Beaumont
'A Practical Guide to Payments for Environmental Services' by Ben Sharples
'A Practical Guide to the Law of Pregnancy and Maternity at Work' by Rebecca Thomas
'A Practical Guide to Redundancy – Second Edition' by Philip Hyland & Collette Moore
'A Practical Guide to International Issues for Scottish Family Lawyers' by Susie Mountain, Donna McKay, Ken MacDonald
'A Practical Guide to the Law on Deprivation of Liberty' by Ben Troke
'A Practical Guide to Rights over Airspace and Subsoil – Second Edition' by Daniel Gatty
'A Practical Guide to the Law in Relation to Inquests' by Ramya Nagesh
'A Practical Guide to the Construction and Rectification of Wills and Trust Instruments (Second Edition)' by Edward Hewitt
'A Practical Guide to Data Protection in Social Housing' by Clare Paterson
'A Practical Guide to Spousal Maintenance – Second Edition' by Liz Cowell
'A Practical Guide to International Parental Child Abduction Law (England and Wales)' by Dr Onyója Momoh
'A Practical Guide to Deprivation of British Citizenship' by Sean Ell
'A Practical Guide to Commercial Property Service Charges' by Rachel Garton
'A Practical Guide to Clinical Negligence – Third Edition' by Geoffrey Simpson-Scott (Geoff)
'A Practical Guide to the Rights of Grandparents in Children Proceedings – Second Edition' by Stuart Barlow

‘The Electronic Communications Code: A Practical Guide – Second Edition’ by Kerry Bretherton KC, James Castle, Mark Loveday

‘A Practical Guide to the Independent School Standards – September 2023 Edition’ by Sarah McKimm

'A Practical Guide to Estate Administration and Crypto Assets' by Richard Marshall

‘A Practical Guide to Parental Alienation in Private and Public Law Children Cases’ by Sam King QC & Frankie Shama

‘Contested Heritage – Removing Art from Land and Historic Buildings’ by Richard Harwood QC, Catherine Dobson, David Sawtell

‘The Limits of Separate Legal Personality: When Those Running a Company Can Be Held Personally Liable for Losses Caused to Third Parties Outside of the Company’ by Dr Mike Wilkinson

‘A Practical Guide to Transgender Law’ by Robin Moira White & Nicola Newbegin

‘A Practical Guide to ‘Stranded Spouses’ in Family Law’ by Mani Singh Basi

‘A Practical Guide to Residential Freehold Conveyancing’ by Lorraine Richardson

‘A Practical Guide to Pensions on Divorce for Lawyers’ by Bryan Scant

‘A Practical Guide to Challenging Sham Marriage Allegations in Immigration Law’ by Priya Solanki

‘A Practical Guide to Digital Communications Evidence in Criminal Law’ by Sam Willis

‘A Practical Guide to Legal Rights in Scotland’ by Sarah-Jane Macdonald

‘A Practical Guide to New Build Conveyancing’ by Paul Sams & Rebecca East

‘A Practical Guide to Inherited Wealth on Divorce’ by Hayley Trim

‘A Practical Guide to Practice Direction 12J and Domestic Abuse in Private Law Children Proceedings’ by Rebecca Cross & Malvika Jaganmohan

‘A Practical Guide to Confiscation and Restraint’ by Narita Bahra QC, John Carl Townsend, David Winch

‘A Practical Guide to the Law of Forests in Scotland’ by Philip Buchan

‘A Practical Guide to Health and Medical Cases in Immigration Law’ by Rebecca Chapman & Miranda Butler

‘A Practical Guide to Bad Character Evidence for Criminal Practitioners by Aparna Rao

‘A Practical Guide to Extradition Law post-Brexit’ by Myles Grandison et al

‘A Practical Guide to Hoarding and Mental Health for Housing Lawyers’ by Rachel Coyle

'Stephens on Contractual Indemnities' by Richard Stephens
'A Practical Guide to the EU Succession Regulation' by Richard Frimston
'A Practical Guide to Solicitor and Client Costs – Second Edition' by Robin Dunne
'Constructive Dismissal – Practice Pointers and Principles' by Benjimin Burgher
'A Practical Guide to Religion and Belief Discrimination Claims in the Workplace' by Kashif Ali
'A Practical Guide to the Law of Medical Treatment Decisions' by Ben Troke
'Fundamental Dishonesty and QOCS in Personal Injury Proceedings: Law and Practice' by Jake Rowley
'A Practical Guide to the Law in Relation to School Exclusions' by Charlotte Hadfield & Alice de Coverley
'A Practical Guide to Divorce for the Silver Separators' by Karin Walker
'The Right to be Forgotten – The Law and Practical Issues' by Melissa Stock
'A Practical Guide to Planning Law and Rights of Way in National Parks, the Broads and AONBs' by James Maurici QC, James Neill et al
'A Practical Guide to Election Law' by Tom Tabori
'A Practical Guide to the Law in Relation to Surrogacy' by Andrew Powell
'A Practical Guide to Claims Arising from Fatal Accidents – Second Edition' by James Patience
'A Practical Guide to Asbestos Claims' by Jonathan Owen & Gareth McAloon
'A Practical Guide to Stamp Duty Land Tax in England and Northern Ireland' by Suzanne O'Hara
'A Practical Guide to the Law of Farming Partnerships' by Philip Whitcomb
'A Practical Guide to the Law of Unlawful Eviction and Harassment – Second Edition' by Stephanie Lovegrove
'A Practical Guide to Costs in Personal Injury Claims – Second Edition' by Matthew Hoe
'A Practical Guide to the General Data Protection Regulation (GDPR) – Second Edition' by Keith Markham
'A Practical Guide to Working with Litigants in Person and McKenzie Friends in Family Cases' by Stuart Barlow
'Protecting Unregistered Brands: A Practical Guide to the Law of Passing Off' by Lorna Brazell
'A Practical Guide to Secondary Liability and Joint Enterprise Post-Jogee' by Joanne Cecil & James Mehigan

'A Practical Guide to the Pre-Action RTA Claims Protocol for Personal Injury Lawyers' by Antonia Ford

'A Practical Guide to Neighbour Disputes and the Law' by Alexander Walsh

'A Practical Guide to Coercive Control for Legal Practitioners and Victims' by Rachel Horman

'A Practical Guide to the Law of Driverless Cars – Second Edition'

by Alex Glassbrook, Emma Northey & Scarlett Milligan

'A Practical Guide to TOLATA Claims' by Greg Williams

'A Practical Guide to Elderly Law – Second Edition' by Justin Patten

'A Practical Guide to Responding to Housing Disrepair and Unfitness Claims' by Iain Wightwick

'A Practical Guide to the Law of Bullying and Harassment in the Workplace' by Philip Hyland

'How to Be a Freelance Solicitor: A Practical Guide to the SRA-Regulated Freelance Solicitor Model' by Paul Bennett

'A Practical Guide to Prison Injury Claims' by Malcolm Johnson

'A Practical Guide to Advising Clients at the Police Station' by Colin Stephen McKeown-Beaumont

'A Practical Guide to Antisocial Behaviour Injunctions – Second Edition' by Iain Wightwick

'Practical Mediation: A Guide for Mediators, Advocates, Advisers, Lawyers, and Students in Civil, Commercial, Business, Property, Workplace, and Employment Cases' by Jonathan Dingle with John Sephton

'The Mini-Pupillage Workbook' by David Boyle

'A Practical Guide to Crofting Law' by Brian Inkster

'A Practical Guide to the Law of Domain Names and Cybersquatting' by Andrew Clemson

'A Practical Guide to the Law of Gender Pay Gap Reporting' by Harini Iyengar

'NHS Whistleblowing and the Law' by Joseph England

'Employment Law and the Gig Economy' by Nigel Mackay & Annie Powell

'A Practical Guide to Noise Induced Hearing Loss (NIHL) Claims' by Andrew Mckie, Ian Skeate, Gareth McAloon

'An Introduction to Beauty Negligence Claims – A Practical Guide for the Personal Injury Practitioner' by Greg Almond

'Intercompany Agreements for Transfer Pricing Compliance' by Paul Sutton

'Zen and the Art of Mediation' by Martin Plowman

'A Practical Guide to Adoption for Family Lawyers' by Graham Pegg

www.ingramcontent.com/pod-product-compliance
Lightning Source LLC
LaVergne TN
LVHW022057200926
848481LV00003B/960
* 9 7 8 1 9 1 6 6 9 8 7 3 4 *